Shetland Bus Man

Shetland Bus Man

Kaare Iversen

The Shetland Times Ltd,
Lerwick.
2004

Shetland Bus Man

ISBN 1 898852 94 4

First published in the UK by Pentland Press Ltd., 2000.
This edition published by The Shetland Times Ltd., 2004.
Reprinted 2010

British Library Cataloguing-in-Publication Data
A catalogue record for this book is available from the British Library.

The publishers would like to thank Willie Smith and
Stephen Howarth for providing additional photographs.

Printed and published by
The Shetland Times Ltd.,
Gremista, Lerwick,
Shetland ZE1 0PX, UK.

Contents

Illustrations

Foreword

I T IS A PLEASURE to write a foreword for Kaare Iversen's book. As a schoolboy during the war I recognised Kaare as one of a large number of Norwegians based in the village, their small fishing boats with the distinctive 'tonk tonk' engines creating a lot of interest. As children we did not realise the importance of their secret comings and goings – an important operation which became known as 'The Shetland Bus'.

It was only after the war that the secret was revealed and the work of the Norwegian freedom fighters became known to the public. They played a decisive role in ending the war, their missions to Norway resulting in a large German army being pinned down to counter the growing resistance movement supplied from Shetland. Because of this the German soldiers in Norway could not be moved to other parts of the war in Europe.

While the story of the Shetland Bus was told by David Howarth, an English officer who was based in Shetland, this is the first time that the story has been told by a Norwegian seaman who was directly involved in the operation and survived, in spite of all the dangers described in this book.

As editor of *Shetland Life* magazine I welcomed Mr Iversen's reminiscences, which created a lot of interest locally. I am sure that this collection, covering the whole of the operation from 1940 to 1945, will find just as great a welcome from a much wider audience. It is also a belated tribute to his many colleagues who died in the operation.

James R. Nicolson

INTRODUCTION

From Fisherman to Fighter

BY TRYGVE SØRVAAG

Trygve Sørvaag is a London-based Norwegian journalist. In 2002 his book, *Shetland Bus – Faces and Places 60 Years On*, was published by The Shetland Times Ltd.

Almost sixty years to the day after the start of the Second World War, I meet Kaare Iversen in Scalloway in Shetland. The retired fisherman from Norway strolls the streets of the town which he has called home since fleeing Nazi-occupied Norway in 1941.

His Norwegian dialect is still strong and distinct – there is almost no hint of the fact that he has lived most of his life abroad. Yet Kaare is not the active youngster he once was. His legs don't work as well as they used to. Nevertheless, he never misses out on his daily rounds. From his council apartment on Gibblestone Court, he often turns towards the museum on Main Street where a small wall of pictures relates the saga of the Norwegians and the Shetland Bus.

It was the German occupation of Norway that brought Kaare Iversen to Shetland. Accompanied by hundreds of other Norwegian fishermen and seamen, he made the small town of a thousand people his base. From here, in the same boats in which they had escaped, the men returned to Norway on clandestine assignments. With them they carried secret agents, saboteurs, weapons, and explosives for the resistance movement, and on the return trip were often refugees. This "traffic",

Introduction

directed by Norwegian "fishing boat soldiers" in a special naval unit, has since been dubbed the Shetland Bus.

Now the streets overflow with memories. Kaare pauses before a large red building dubbed the "Norwegian House". Here lived several men from the crews. Across the street is a workshop and the slip where boats lay moored while awaiting orders to head to Norway. On the wall, a small sign reminds visitors that Crown Prince Olav opened this Norwegian slipway in 1942. Further up the hill is the building which housed the local café – or "canteen", as the Shetlanders called it.

"Sunday evenings we used to go to the café to talk to the local girls," says Kaare. Which sheds some light on why he is still in Shetland long after the others left for home in 1945. Scarcely one year earlier, he wed Christina – one of the local girls who worked at the café.

After the war, Kaare and Christina were a living testament to the difficult times that resulted in lasting relations between two coastal peoples – a modern variant of the staunch ties Norway and Shetland have enjoyed since the first Vikings set foot on their shores more than one thousand years ago.

Since his wife passed away in 1973, Kaare has lived alone in Scalloway, yet it was never an option to move back to Norway. Despite attempting to move back Norway just after the war, he was just unable to settle in. In 1951, Kaare returned his Norwegian passport. Shetland had become his new home.

In his living room, Kaare Iversen serves coffee and biscuits to visitors who come to hear his stories. On the wall pictures of his family and fishing boats share space with a large map, its arrows indicating many of his 50-plus military missions to Norway as a Shetland Bus man. The county shield of Flatanger stands on a shelf as a reminder of the home he left behind, and a picture of a whaling crew depicts the life that awaited him after the war's end.

He is dumbfounded by my query as to how, a mere 23 years old, he could risk his life as a combatant on the Shetland Bus. How could

Kaare at home. Photo © Trygve Sørvaag.

anybody think up such an ignorant question? Nevertheless, he answers me:

"I wanted to inflict as much harm as possible on the Germans and the Quislings. They came into our land like scoundrels. That was my motivation." To understand, we must travel back in time.

When the war began in Norway on the 9th of April 1940, Kaare Iversen was a typical teenager living on the coast. He had been in the fishing industry since he was knee-high, he had crewed cargo ships, and he had worked as a mechanic on the local pilot boat. Just before the war broke out, his family purchased a new fishing smack, and Kaare Iversen had realised that the sea would be his life. This was the way of things on the coast at that time, and this was the way in Flatanger in North-Trøndlag. The sea set limits, and the sea created possibilities.

The unexpected invasion changed all this. Soldiers in the streets and the German occupation of Norway made many young men in the land uneasy. Kaare Iversen was one of several thousand young men who

Introduction

decided to flee the country. His goal was to cross the North Sea and return with the Englishmen to force the Germans out.

In his family's fishing boat, Kaare set out on a hazardous journey across the North Sea to Shetland. From here he was sent further by boat and train to the British capital. He remembers well the day he stood in the centre of London for the first time. Everything was new and exciting. So different from the small coastal community he had grown up in. Now he only awaited assignment to a branch of the military. Then came the inquiry as to whether he would meet Martin Linge – the Norwegian actor and resistance man who had built up a special Norwegian unit in England, Company Linge.

Linge often chose fishermen and seamen for this special clandestine unit, and Kaare Iversen was perfect for the job. Kaare had little idea what the unit actually did, but nonetheless began service as an SOE-agent in the navy's special division – what towards the end of the war would be labelled the "Royal Norwegian Naval Special Unit" – or more popularly, the Shetland Bus. Kaare was sent back to Shetland, from where he undertook more than fifty military missions back to Norway.

When Kaare Iversen was discharged from the Norwegian navy in June of 1946, he returned to the life of a fisherman. He subsequently spent years on whaling crews in South Georgia in the South Atlantic Ocean.

Many years passed before Kaare Iversen was ready to look back on his war years, but in the 1970s he began to put his stories down on paper. Almost thirty years later, these stories were printed as a long series of articles in the periodical Shetland Life, and a few years ago the stories were released in book format for the first time. But this is the first time his stories have been made available for a broader readership.

In this book, Kaare Iversen relates his wartime experiences in his own words. He recounts his flight from Norway, his arrival in London, how he became a Shetland Bus man, and how he sailed some fifty perilous assignments to Norway during the war. The result is an intensely personal rendering of a story we know from other books, but this is how Kaare Iversen experienced these events in retrospect, years after the war. He delivers a personal and stirring contribution to those accounts we have already heard.

Kaare Iversen (born 10.10.1918) died in Shetland in August of 2001, 82 years old. He left behind a Norwegian-Shetland family of three surviving daughters, fourteen grandchildren, and thirteen great-grandchildren.

One of 3300 Norwegian refugees

Kaare Ivesen was only one of nearly 3300 Norwegian refugees, transported on approximately 300 boats over the North Sea during the war. From the west coast of Norway, England was the goal, even though most boats landed in Shetland first as it was the closest.

That the seafarers first headed for Shetland was hardly a coincidence. As fishermen home in Norway, crossing the North Sea was not unusual; they were, therefore well acquainted with the route to the island realm in the west. The fishers knew that Shetland lay only a day away if wind and weather allowed it, something far from certain.

Kaare standing at the slip in Scalloway. Photo © Trygve Sørvaag.

Introduction

The Norwegians also knew that in Shetland were a people with which they had much in common. Much of the explanation lies in the fact that, until 500 years ago, the Shetland Islands belonged to Norway. Shetlanders know this. And if they could choose, they would much rather be Norwegian than Scottish – not to mention British. Norwegian war refugees came to a people who themselves felt Norwegian. Numerous Shetland dialect words originate in Norwegian, and nigh on all of the place-names stem from the Norwegian Vikings. As if that weren't enough, new research reveals that at least 60 percent of the population of Shetland stems from Norwegian Vikings. These were no strangers who welcomed the Norwegian refugees. They were family.

The first boats set off for Great Britain, or England as people then said, already in the spring and early summer of 1940. The short-lived battle against the invading Germans was over in Norway, and many wished to do what the king and government already had done: Leave for London to continue the campaign in exile.

It was mostly young, unmarried men who made the crossing. Several of them had taken part in the fighting in Norway, and they now wished to enlist in the Norwegian forces being built up in Great Britain. Other simply got caught up in englandsfeber (England fever) which raged the Norwegian coast early in the war. People left because so many had already done the same, or due to a heartfelt desire to be a part of what was happening in England – without quite knowing what it was this activity might involve.

Later in the war, the refugee traffic changed character as steadily more had to flee the country after participating in resistance work. Not infrequently, entire families had to escape over the North Sea. At this time, groups of resistance workers had been organised into a system providing hiding places and sea transport. These were referred to as "export groups".

Most made the journey in fishing vessels of various types, but there were also those who went in small motor boats, sailboats, row boats and the like. Often neighbours and friends worked together, acquired a vessel, and in all secrecy pointed their bow westwards under the cover of night.

The trip over the North Sea was far from safe. To begin with, it was important that escape plans did not get out. This would have stopped many of the youngest refugees, who only rarely informed parents or friends of their plans, but those who suddenly discovered an empty bed in the boys' room were seldom in doubt about where their son was headed. In some places, people talked about England as if it was an island out in the archipelago.

Even more crucial was it that families were in no way involved. It was illegal to assist such activities, and there were several cases in which parents of refugees were taken hostage in an attempt to frighten others who might be considering leaving the country. In 1941, the Germans declared all aiding of refugees to the United Kingdom punishable by death.

The Germans went to great pains to put a stop to the North Sea crossings, and the long coastline was patrolled from land, sea, and air. Although the refugees often felt that the greatest threat was that of the German patrols and their Norwegian informers, it was the North Sea that posed the worst danger. Few of the vessels used were constructed for such journeys, and the storms of autumn and winter gave them serious problems. It is estimated that the sea took 160 lives, from refugees in row boats to those who embarked on large cutters.

Those who managed to come ashore in Shetland were immediately put into the hands of the authorities. The refugees were watched over by the military, and considered suspicious until confirmation had been received that they were not German spies. In Shetland, the refugees were sent to refugee camps in Lerwick where the Norwegian consulate coordinated their further transport to London – under constant military guard.

Kaare Iversen and James R. Nicolson in the Scalloway Museum.
Photo © Trygve Sørvaag.

In London, together with all the others war refugees who had enter the United Kingdom, the Norwegians were escorted to the Royal Victoria Patriotic School. After a thorough interrogation, most were freed of all suspicion and assigned to one of the branches of the Norwegian armed forces.

Most entered the Norwegian merchant marine, the air force, the navy, or the army - which was at that time being built up in the United Kingdom. Women refugees usually served in one of the numerous Norwegian institutions established in the UK. Such work could take the form of a teaching position at the Norwegian school, or a secretary at one of the many Norwegian offices. Many women also worked at the Norwegian hotels in London.

Very few of the refugees were singled out for special service. These were called up by Martin Linge – the Norwegian actor and resistance man who trained a special Norwegian unit in England, Company Linge, in cooperation with the SOE (Special Operations Executive).

The idea was brilliant. Norwegian fishers and seamen who had just arrived in fishing boats were specially trained in marksmanship and sabotage. They were then sent back to Norway on the same fishing boats. When they appeared on the fishing grounds in the morning together with all the other fishing boats, nothing distinguished them from the other fishermen and boats, despite having a completely different sort of "catch" in mind. They were agents on special assignment, behind enemy lines.

The initiative for the secret operations came from the British authorities who, already in the summer of 1940, had perceived the usefulness of some of the refugees and their boats for military purposes. In addition to being skilled seafarers, they were intimately familiar with the coast, and their boats had the advantage of being able to easily blend in with other fishing vessels. The British boats, personnel, and leadership shared none of these advantages. The goal was to contact what resistance organisations and groups might exist, supply them with what they needed in the way of weapons and equipment, and give them instructions and training. If possible, the boats were to return carrying refugees.

After Martin Linge had chosen his men from the refugees in London, they were sent to the British for training. In the space of a few months, the Norwegian fishermen were to be transformed to soldiers.

After intensive preparation in areas including marksmanship, sabotage, and hand-to-hand combat, the uniformed fishermen were transferred to the base in Shetland. From here, missions to Norway were organised by the British military in close cooperation with Norwegian authorities.

Until the autumn of 1943, the traffic was carried out on ordinary fishing boats equipped only with simple machine guns. As the Germans became increasing aware of the operation, the slow-going boats became too dangerous and the losses too many. Salvation appeared in the form of three swift and well-equipped submarine chasers. These naval vessels were normally used to hunt submarines, but three such boats were revamped and delivered to the Shetland Bus by the American navy. As a result, the Shetland Bus could continue its transportation of agents, military equipment, and refugees even after the fishing boats had outspent their role.

According to the Shetland base's own figures, the sub-chasers Hessa, Hitra, and Vigra completed a total of 120 tours between Norway and Shetland from November 1943 to the war's end. One hundred agents were landed on the Norwegian coast, and 200 agents and refugees transported back to Shetland. After the three sub-chasers were put into service, the Shetland Bus crew did not lose a single man or boat. All told, the Shetland Bus transported 192 agents and 383 tons of military equipment to the Norwegian coast in the course of the war, bringing 73 agents and 373 refugees back with them.

After the war, the stories of the uniformed fishers of the Shetland Bus have been the stuff of much attention, legend, and "hero worship", in the form of books and films. Especially one of the skippers has stood as a representative for them all – Shetlands-Larsen, or Leif Andreas Larsen as he is really called. In Norway, his name has become virtually synonymous with the Shetland Bus.

Kaare Iversen was one of the approximately one hundred other fishermen and seamen who stood shoulder to shoulder with Shetlands-Larsen on the legendary boats. He is one of the many silent voices and anonymous faces who for many years uttered as little as possible about their war-time experiences. This was how they had been trained. Silence was a virtue.

Consequently, most of the Norwegians who crossed the North Sea during the war were forgotten. Quietly and unobserved, they returned to their anonymous existences – just as they had been before they had made the crossing. They were neither heroes nor villains. They simply went on with their lives as if nothing had happened.

CHAPTER ONE

Across the North Sea

I WAS BORN at Ivorden, Flatanger, in Norway in 1918, and grew up on a pilot station where my father, Rudolf Iversen, was a pilot.

I started school in 1925 at the age of seven, which was the normal age in Norway, and finished school in 1933, when I was 15. In July of the same year I started work on the pilot-boat along with my father and the other pilot on the station, and continued there until September 1936. At that point I went to college for six months, then went to the salmon fishing in the summer of 1937, changing to halibut fishing during the ensuing winter. The years 1938/39 followed the same pattern, but I returned to the pilot-boat in the spring of 1939, and was there until Christmas of that year.

It was after that that I got a berth on a purse-net boat fishing for winter herring on Norway's west coast. When the Second World War started in September 1939, there was the immediate hazard of drifting mines and crews had to keep a sharp lookout, as numerous mines had been observed on the fishing grounds. At the end of the winter season the boat went back to her home port and the crew were paid off. It was on the passage back that I contracted a bad cold which developed into pneumonial bronchitis, and I became very ill, so much so that the doctor expressed doubts as to whether I would recover. He was wrong, and when I was up and about again I signed on a small coaster of about 200 tons.

When I came ashore again the hated Germans had occupied Norway for three months. I worked on several temporary jobs, all the time on the lookout for someone who might join me in some sabotage work against the enemy, but I had no luck.

Then I got a berth on a fishing boat that was going to fish cod at the Lofoten Islands and we set off in the first week of February 1941. On this trip I had the opportunity to take note of places where the Germans had started to build gun forts, and I stored away this information. At the end of April I was back home and went salmon fishing with my father in the summer of 1941.

Villa Island. The author's home.

My father and I had a fishing boat between us. She was 42 feet overall. After the salmon fishing finished I went to a slipway with the boat to get the engine overhauled and have her painted, so that boat and engine would be in good order when I decided to escape to Britain. I had been thinking about this for some time, but the snag was – who would take a chance and come with me? There were a few boys the same age as myself who were talking about escape, but not to Britain. They would rather go to Sweden, but that didn't fit with my plan. I think the Germans and the local quisling were keeping an eye on me, but they took no action.

In August 1941, I got news that two Norwegians and a Swede had to get out of Norway, so I got the boat ready to go with them. Three boys came to the pilot station, but it was difficult to get enough fuel oil and lubricating oil. To get the oil you needed to have coupons, and my father and I had only enough to get about 400 litres of fuel and about 15 litres of lubricating oil. That was not enough to start a voyage of 400-500 miles. So I took the *Villa* with the three boys on board and steamed about 25-30 miles along the coast to a merchant I knew, for I was pretty sure he would let me have the fuel I needed. When we got there we found that the merchant was away on a business trip, and only his wife and daughter were at home.

I had to tell them why I had come. I explained that I had coupons for only 400 litres of fuel oil and a small amount of lubricating oil, but what I really wanted was 800-1000 litres of fuel oil and 40 litres of lubricating oil, and I had enough cash to pay for that quantity.

When the good lady heard the quantity I wanted, she said, "Are you going to England?" I said, "Yes, if I get the oil."

The daughter said to her mother, "Give the boy the oil. I know if daddy had been home he would have given him what he is asking for. When this boy had his boat on the slipway this summer daddy asked him why he was having the engine overhauled, and the boy replied that it was a good policy to keep boat and engine in good order. Daddy had said, jokingly, 'If you are going to England then come here and I will give you fuel and I will come with you'."

I got the fuel oil and when we were filling the fuel tank and fuel barrels in the hold, German soldiers stood on the quay watching us. One of the Germans said to the quay foreman, "This fishing boat is too small to go to England." The foreman replied that the boat was to go to the north of Norway for the herring fishing. I got a lot of rationed goods at the shop, but they couldn't give me lubricating oil as they had none, so I had to return home.

On the way back we found ourselves in the middle of a German convoy for about half an hour, but we excited no interest. When I got home I went to another merchant and asked if he could supply me with the lubricating. This time the answer was, "Yes." But he did more than that. He insisted that I took two barrels of fuel oil as a gift from him because I was taking the chance to go to England. I didn't tell him that I was going to be heading for Shetland.

I now had fuel, luboil and stores to last us for a month, but I had no chart for the North Sea. One of the Norwegian lifeboats at the pilot station was a boat called the *Gustav Bull*, and I knew all the crew. The skipper asked me if I had a chart for the North Sea, and when I admitted that I didn't he gave me one of his after he had erased the boat's name from it.

Now I was ready to start the journey to the unknown, and I was the only one of the four of us who had ever been to sea. One of the Norwegian boys was a policeman, while the other had been a sergeant in the Royal Guard; and the Swede, we did not know what he was – he certainly was a strange sort of a stranger.

The Germans had an armed whale-catcher as a patrol boat outside the pilot station, but the patrol boat did not stay out on patrol after dark so I sent my young brother up the hill to see where it went in to anchor. At 8pm the patrol boat went off duty so the coast was clear for us to go. People on the pilot station gave us a good send-off, but my father was not there as he had gone away on a business trip. So if there were questions as to where the boat and I had gone, he did not know; the story was that I was somewhere up to the north of Norway.

I started the engine and took the *Villa* away from the quay. It was 9.15pm on 19th August, 1941 – not yet quite dark, but dark enough. The journey had started.

For the first five hours we steamed west-north-west in order to get out of sight of land. The weather was just right – a slight north-north-east breeze. We had our breakfast on deck, and set watches, but I had to be up all the time to check the course and see that the engine had

4

enough luboil. I also transferred the fuel oil from the barrels in the hold to the fuel tank in the engine room.

Kaare Iversen in the wheelhouse of *Villa*.
Photo taken by 'the swede' as they escaped from Norway.

The first two days passed in perfect weather conditions. We were now somewhere west of Ålesund. On Sunday morning we were some distance farther south, and at 10am were only about 10 miles off land. We saw four German patrol boats or minesweepers, but they paid no attention to us. We kept going on a south-west course, and the wind began to freshen a bit, but not too much, so at 12 midday we hoisted the mainsail, jib and mizzen. The boat's speed increased very markedly, and she didn't roll so much, but at 3.10pm, as I was coming out of the engine-room, I saw through the wheelhouse door that a German flying-boat was coming straight for us.

At the time two of us were down in the engine-room, two in the forward cabin. After the first burst of gunfire I went up on deck and released all the halliards to let the sails drop to the deck, then went back down to the engine-room. The Germans continued shooting at us for over 20 minutes. Their gunfire riddled the wheelhouse, and they holed the boat just above the water line with their shelling. Whenever we rolled a big rush of water came into the hold. The flying boat tried to land, but the sea was too rough, so they gave up the attempt. The German bastards left us.

Villa was just drifting. The mizzen sail had not fallen all the way down when I released the halliard, but had stuck halfway down the mast. We put pieces of sacking and grease with pieces of plank over the shell holes, and stowed away the sails. The mizzen had got the worst of it – the shooting had left it hanging in strips.

We set course again for Shetland and drove the engine to its maximum. I was in the engine-room from 4pm on Saturday until 5pm on Sunday. When I felt like falling asleep I took a small glass of navy rum. We had a dozen bottles on board. On Sunday afternoon, about 5.30pm, the engine stopped without warning. I went down to see what was wrong and found a fuel-pipe fractured. I had a spare pipe, but that had to be softened before I could put it on. When I had managed to get it fitted, I started the engine, and steamed away at full speed. I noticed that there was a lot of seaweed drifting near us and the sea was as smooth as a tabletop, so I knew that we were not far from land.

After steaming for about an hour and a half I heard a hissing sound from the engine-room. When I looked down I saw sparks coming from the hot bulb on the cylinder head. I stopped the engine, changed the joint on the hot bulb, and started up again. For sure, after just half an hour, the same thing happened again. I stopped, changed the joint, started the engine, but this time, instead of giving her full speed, I set her to slow ahead and changed course south-south-west.

We had a good meal and a dram. The two Norwegian boys had locked the Swede down in the forward cabin because it was his job to do the washing up. After he had finished we let him up on deck. He told us that he had 40 pounds in English notes, and whoever saw land first would get the money. We were dodging until about 4am in the morning – it was 24th August – and I put the engine to full ahead and changed course to south-west.

At 6am I was up on top of the wheelhouse when I spotted land to the west of us. I went down into the wheelhouse and altered course to due west, steamed for another hour, then told the boy who was on watch with me that I had seen land an hour ago. I pointed the land out for him. He went forward to the cabin and shouted the good news to the other two boys. We were very glad that we had made land. We knew that it was somewhere in Shetland – but where? There was only one thing to do – put two of the boys ashore. We found a perfect place and the policeman and the Swede were landed. They found an old rowing boat hauled up on the beach, managed to launch it and came back to us. We had dropped anchor and stopped the engine, ready to go ashore and find out how far from Lerwick we were, and to find a pilot to take us there.

The four of us went ashore in the rowing boat, two pulling on the oars and two bailing with buckets, as the old boat was leaking badly. We made the beach and pulled the boat clear from the water, then began to walk up through some fields. We came to a farmhouse and the Swede asked what island we were on. The lady of the house told us we were on an island called Fetlar, and that our fishing boat was at anchor at Sandwick.

The old lady asked us to come into her house where we met her daughter. She was setting a table and prepared a lovely meal for us. I told the Swede to tell her not to bother as we had just had our breakfast before we came into the bay. But all in vain – we had to sit down and take the food that was placed in front of us.

When we first came to the house we met a young man who was cutting grass, but he had disappeared. After we had our meal, the old lady asked if we would like to have a shave and clean up, so we said through the Swede that that was very good of her, and we sent two of the boys back to the *Villa* to bring some towels, shaving gear and a camera. We had a shave and cleaned up.

When we came out of the house we met two men in army uniforms. One of them, as we got to know, was a sergeant in the Home Guard, and the other was a boy about the same age as we were. I am not quite sure what the boy's name was, but I think it was Frederick F. Johnson. The sergeant was Bruce something. We were ordered to go back to the *Villa* and wait until the duty boat came along to take us to Lerwick. We had the Home Guard men on board with us for two days, so to break the monotony I started the engine, we pulled up the anchor and took the two of them for a run. They really enjoyed that. On the second day, after we had stripped and stored away sails and running gear, we were told that the duty boat was coming to take us to Lerwick.

The boat duly arrived, and we saw that it was an ordinary fishing boat. When she came close enough for us to read it, we saw her name was *Heather Bell* from Whalsay. That was my first experience of Shetland or Scottish fishing boats. She was to tow us to Lerwick. Our engine was running so it was not much towing for the *Heather Bell* to do – she simply made sure we were following. We went through Whalsay Sound and when we were opposite the Whalsay harbour the Swede came up on deck with a tin can in his hand. He came into the wheelhouse and asked me for some nuts and bolts to put in it. I asked what it was he had in the can. "Forty forged English pounds," he replied. He got the nuts and bolts, put them in the can, hammered down the top then dumped it over the side. The other two boys didn't have much use for the Swede, and neither did I. We just tolerated him.

We arrived in Lerwick and berthed at the old fish market. The two Norwegian boys and the Swede were taken ashore by the immigration people, and our gear was also removed. But I had to take the *Villa* to another berth, and two immigration men accompanied me. I could not speak much English, and they could speak no Norwegian, but we got to a quay and moored the boat. I did not like the quay, as a strong wind and a rough sea were lying right on to it, and I only had two fenders, which were certainly not enough. I took the jib and the mizzens, which were folded up, put a rope around each sail and used them as fenders. The sails were really for no more use as they were riddled with machine-gun bullets.

I locked up the wheelhouse and the forward cabin and was then taken ashore to the Customs and immigration officers. They searched all of our gear, broke ordinary pencils in two pieces, looked through letters that we had in our wallets and took our cigarettes. On top of my suitcase I had a Colt .32 caliber pistol and a Norwegian sports knife. One of the other boys had two bottles of Advocaat. The old Customs officer took the two bottles and opened them, smelled the neck of each bottle, then set up two glasses and told the owner of the bottles to fill the two glasses and drink one of them. The boy did so and the officer watched to see if the drink had any ill effect. When he saw that the boy was all right, he put the corks back in the bottles and put them in his pocket. The four of us had a good laugh about it all.

When we finished with the Customs and immigration people, we were taken to a hut and put in a big, bare room with two double bunks. It was to be two boys to a bunk. After we went to bed we started to talk about what they had taken from us. The Swede said that he had only one condom left, and they had taken even that. The other three of us had also had all our gear taken from us. We were supposed to get it all back when we got to London. The four of us were talking a lot of rubbish. We thought we heard somebody sniggering or laughing, but we were not sure. At last we all fell asleep.

We were wakened at 6am in the morning and went for a wash and a shave. We had come back to our room when a door leading into it opened and three young Norwegian girls came out of the adjoining room. We greeted them with a cheery 'good morning' and got the same greeting in reply. After they left, we four boys cleared up, folded our blankets and pillowcases then went for breakfast. After breakfast, when we were sitting outside the hut, two immigration men asked for the Swede. They used a name we didn't recognize. They asked for a Gustav Warholm, but we had known him as Kare Anker. When he turned up they took him away with them. We all wondered why he was being taken away, but the men wouldn't tell us. It took me four years to find out the reason.

A man from the Norwegian Consul in Lerwick came to the immigration camp and asked the men who had brought fishing boats from Norway to Shetland if their boats could do a trip from Shetland to Buckie. There were three fishing boats to take all the refugees of whom there were now 101. My boat was the smallest, so I took 13 other boys, which gave us a total of 16. And what boys they were! They cared not for God or the devil. Most of them had come from Bergen in a small fishing boat 30 feet long. After they came into Lerwick they stopped pumping and the boat just sank to the bottom.

The three fishing boats that left Lerwick were, *Solveig,* which was the biggest, *Klippen,* next biggest and the *Villa,* the smallest. The senior skipper got a sealed sailing order after we had loaded our stores. We had had a lot of tinned meat on our boat, but the men who searched our ship destroyed all our tinned stores.

Before we could start on our journey we had to clean up the cabin. I had had a good sleeping bag and that was cut pieces. Speaking about vandals today – well, they were on the go 50 years ago, and they were not teenagers, but fully grown men who should have had more sense and responsibility.

At last everyone was on board and we set off first, then the *Solveig* and lastly the *Klippen.* We left Lerwick about 6pm. The *Solveig* and the *Villa* kept together while the *Klippen* disappeared to the east. I signalled to the *Solveig* that I would come alongside her so that I could talk to the skipper. I suggested that, as we were not allowed to use navigation lights, I thought it would be a good idea to put a heavy rope between the two ships. I had a heavy coir rope about 50 fathoms long, so we put that out, and it proved of help to the *Solveig* just two hours later. I saw the rope jumping just abreast of us and then disappearing astern. I slowed down and told the boys to take in the slack as I came astern, until we could see the *Solveig*. We were only about 20 feet from her when the skipper shouted to me that they had got a blocked fuel line.

The *Villa* towed the *Solveig* three times that night – about six hours' towing in all – and in the morning after daylight the *Solveig* slowed down so that we could come alongside about 15 feet apart. *Solveig's* skipper asked me what course I had been steering compared to him, so I told him my compass reading.

Both compasses were just about the same, but there might have been a big difference if the two boats were lying alongside each other. We decided to carry on, and the first land we saw after Shetland was Noss Head, though we did not know that at the time. We steamed along in fine smooth sea and soaring sun until we saw a fishing boat, and steamed towards her, asking how far it was to Buckie. The skipper on the Scots fishing boat told us that we had to cross the Moray Firth and the high cliff we saw in the distance was Noss Head. He told us that there was a beacon in the Moray Firth and our best chance was to try to find that and stay there until morning, as we didn't have a chance of getting into Buckie that night. We thanked them for their help and started off.

It is an old saying that the devil looks after his own, and we came right over to the beacon and stopped there. The skipper of the *Solveig* took his boat right alongside the *Villa*, and asked if we had plenty of drinking water. We had two or three barrels, and we transferred one barrel so that our neighbors could make some coffee. After the two ships' crews had had a meal and cleaned up, out came two guitars and an accordion, and we had some music. On board the *Solveig* were five or six young girls. The boat's deck was big enough to have a dance, so we started dancing and singing, but of course always watching for aircraft. Nobody wanted to stop, so it was between three and four in the morning when we started for Buckie.

We arrived in Buckie about 7.30am, packed our belongings and locked up our fishing boats before handing the keys over to the Norwegian Consul's men in Buckie. The *Klippen* was the last one to come in. She had steamed a distance of over 285 miles from Lerwick to Buckie. Our two boats had taken a straight course from Fair Isle to the Pentland Skerries, but the tide had pulled us too far east, so we had not seen the Skerries.

In Buckie we were marched up to the town hall where we got a good meal, and out came the accordion, the two guitars and a fiddle. There was also a piano in the town hall and the dancing started again. There were now nine young girls and three older women and they all enjoyed a dance.

From Buckie we went to Aberdeen where we were put into the Douglas Hotel for a night and a day. We were not allowed to go to the public bar or the lounge, so if we wanted a drink it was brought to a big meeting room that was for our use. I went for a shower and I had just turned it on when someone came and knocked on the bathroom door, shouting something about a blackout. I just opened the door and a young girl was standing there. She was one of the hotel staff and she came in and checked the bathroom curtain. I just stood there and watched what she did. I had a towel round my waist so I was decent enough.

The young girl spoke away, I think about the bloody Germans, but I could not understand very much of what she said. She stopped speaking when we heard the explosion of the bombs, which were dropped near Aberdeen Harbour. She left the bathroom so that I could finish taking my shower.

The following evening we were marched to Aberdeen Railway Station and put on a train for King's Cross. That was the Saturday and we arrived at King's Cross on the Sunday morning. The women and two or three children were taken away to a refugee camp and the men were taken to a girls' school. There were not very many girls there, perhaps about a dozen.

When the two boys who had come across with me got our sleeping quarters arranged we went to the cafeteria for something to eat as we had missed our breakfast. And what did we see? The bloody Swede, sitting along with some other Norwegian. We went over to speak to him but the bastard did not want to speak to us, so we left him alone.

Every day after we had arrived in Shetland each of us got one pound spending money. That was for cigarettes and whatever you wanted, so as we steamed from Shetland to Buckie we had some money. My two Norwegian friends found some other Norwegians and started to play a game of poker. The newfound Norwegians asked Thorleif and Brynjar about which boat they had come across in so they told them the name of the boat. When they heard that, they told them what the Swede had been telling them. Well, my friends told them the right story from when we started from Norway until we landed in Shetland.

One day I was sitting in the canteen talking to one of the boys from the *Solveig* when the Swede came over and asked if I could give him five pounds, because he had lost all his money playing poker with some South American. I told him that after all he had told here at the camp, about what he had done to take three stupid Norwegian boys across the North Sea without any help from the stupid boys, the answer to his request was NO. He tried the same thing with the others, Thorleif and Brynjar, but he just got the same result from them. When the refugees found out about him he was more or less boycotted. Very few would talk to him.

Thorleif, Brynjar and I were at the camp for 10 days because of the Swede. The security people found out something about him and that delayed our release. When we did get out the Swede was still at the camp and I heard that he had been sent over to Canada to work in a lumber camp.

Well Thorleif, Brynjar and I were now free to go to the armed forces, or for my part the Norwegian Merchant Navy, but it did not work out that way. After we left the refugee camp we were taken to an office at Pall Mall where we met Captain Nagel, one of the organisers for hit and run units. In that office we were asked a lot of questions about German movements in our part of Norway, so we told them what we knew. After Captain Nagel, the three of us met Captain Martin Linge. He told us that he wanted us to work for him and his unit. Captain Linge told us about how to sabotage German offices and also plant explosives, in ships and near fuel tanks, with time fuses. It sounded very exciting and not too dangerous either, because you planted your demolition charges and set the time fuses. The way he told it to us sounded easy. The three of us joined what was called Linge Company and the next was to get to the training camps, but before that we had to wait about one week.

The first night out of the refugee camp the three of us were put into a hotel at Piccadilly. I cannot remember the name. I went out alone because Thorleif and Brynjar wanted to go to a corner house for a meal. I wanted to look around a bit so I was left alone. I came past a fun fair or something like that, so I went in and to my delight I spotted the air gun stall. I got my air gun and started shooting, but the gun I got was one of those that fired around the corner, so you might get the pellet you thought you fired at the target in your neck instead. I got another gun and it was a good one. I got three prizes but they were no use to me so I handed them back.

Fed up with shooting, I went to a machine where you worked a crane and grab for cigarettes, etc. I got 180 cigarettes and an electric shaver. I handed the shaver back and got 10 shillings.

When I was standing at the machine a man came up to me and started to speak Norwegian to me. He asked how long I had been in London, when I had come from Norway and was I going to the armed Norwegian forces or to the Norwegian Merchant Navy. I told him that I had been over for a few days. I also told him that I was going to the merchant navy. He spoke to me for a few minutes after that, and then he left.

I did not like being spoken to in a place like that. I kept playing one machine after the other and then I landed back at the shooting range. I got the good gun again and I was doing fine when this little fat man came and stood beside me. He started to speak Norwegian to me so I answered politely to his questions, which were just about the same as the first man's. After I had shot about five rounds he asked me if I would like to go for a drink. I told him I did not drink (which was a lie) so he left me.

Well, I was not going to stay there and be involved with another Norwegian-speaking man so I went to the entrance and waited until a lot of people were going out and I got right in the middle of them. I made my way back to the hotel and had to ring the doorbell before the door was opened.

One of the Norwegian-speaking men appeared and asked if I would invite him in. I said no, I was not allowed to take anyone into the hotel with me. Well, I got in and into my room. Thorleif and Brynjar were already in and asked what I had done. I told them and then they told me that something similar had happened to them. We decided not to say anything to Captain Linge's office.

The next morning we went down to Pall Mall to Captain Linge's office where we met one of the staff, a Sergeant Steneson, and he told us that Captain Linge would be in soon. When Captain Linge came in he greeted us with, "Good morning." He asked what we had done last night, so we told him but did not mention the two Norwegian-speaking men.

Captain Linge told us that we had to move from the hotel we were in and go to a hotel west of Gloucester Underground Station – Hotel Barkley I think it was. Then he said, "I wonder which one of you is going to the merchant navy." Of course it could only be me. Then he said that the man who had spoken to us was put out to see if we would tell what armed forces or merchant navy we would join. To say the merchant navy was okay because most of the Norwegians were more or less attached to the sea. Captain Linge was pleased with us for not saying that we were members of Captain Linge's company.

We were at the Barkley Hotel for two days and then were moved again to a small village on the Thames where we stayed in a bungalow. It was called Water Lodge and every evening, when the river patrol came past the house they shouted, "Water Lodge on." All the doors and windows were completely covered, but when we got outside we saw a light shining through a crack in the wall. We managed to repair it so that sorted the blackout problem.

We were at Water Lodge for a whole week and we had a good time, but all of us wanted to get to the training camps. Then one day we got the order that we would move out next morning. All of us were in quite good spirits, bar the woman who kept house for us. I cannot remember her name. All the boys just called her Mum.

The next morning we took all our belongings and went over the Thames and got into the truck that was to take us to the training camp. On the road to the camp we had to go to an army depot to get uniforms to be dressed as soldiers. We were on the road for about three or four hours when we came to a big mansion. It was sitting in a big park with rose beds and lots of flowers. The place was called Stoddon Park – likely a name given for the duration of the war – and the nearest railway station was called Liz. We were shown to our sleeping quarters and told to change into our uniforms and put all our civilian clothes away. As we were now soldiers, we were shown how to make up our beds and how to lay out our kits, etc.

The following morning we were called up at 5.30am. We shaved, dressed, made our beds and then went down in front lane for an inspection. We had square drill for half an hour then put gas masks on for inspection and testing. We ran about 100 yards, then the sergeant took a twist on the air hose of the gas mask to see if they were fitting tight on our faces. We were dismissed at 6pm, got a cup of tea, then were called back on line at 6.30am. We did a quick march around the woods until 7.30am.

Well, I can only say that the first two or three days were pure hell on our feet and legs. Our brand new hob-nailed boots were as stiff as a board and we were marching through the woods on uneven ground. But it was also a lot of fun. We got lessons in what was called silent killing and also ju-jitsu. However the most important was how to blow up railways and bridges, fuel tanks and water posts in power stations.

We got to know different types of fuse to be used in different jobs. It was very interesting. We also had chart reading and out in the fields we learned Morse and semaphore, plus a few hours of basic navigation. We had strict physical training every day in the forenoon. We had to climb up a platform above a sandpit and jump from there. We started first from a platform about six feet from the ground and that was nothing so we were ordered to the next stage – 12 feet – and that was the limit. We did not break any ankles, arms or necks, but we did get a lot of bruises. It was good fun. There were 28 Norwegians and as many British staff.

Every Thursday afternoon we were allowed to go to the town, Petersfield. My pal and I used to go to the canteen, home from home, we had a good laugh. Sometimes the old woman who worked there noticed us as soon as we went in. We did not have any regimental marks or any badges showing, nor nationality marks, absolutely nothing and we could not speak much English. What English we did pick up from the soldiers was not very nice to use in a canteen or shop, so we were careful what we said. We always carried an English-Norwegian phrase book and also a Norwegian-English dictionary, so we did not embarrass any of the old ladies at the canteen.

I remember one Sunday my pal and I went into the canteen and this lady came to us and took us by the arm and walked us over to a table where two Wrens were sitting. We understood that the lady had found out that we were two Norwegian seamen who had joined the army so she thought it was all right for her to introduce us to the Wrens. Well, the Wrens did not object, so we had tea and cakes with the two girls then went to a lake and hired two rowing boats. We split up, my pal with one girl and I with the other. It was a very enjoyable afternoon. After we came ashore we went back to a cafe for a meal and after that went to a cinema. I suppose the film was okay but I will say it is not a film that I would go and see twice. I think that was the same opinion as the Wrens. We had to be back at camp before 10pm so we did not have much time to say good night and arrange another date for the next Sunday, but we managed it.

Back at camp some of the other boys had seen us in the company of the Royal Navy so we were ragged about it. They said it was a good job that the Wrens did not have torpedoes, but they might have something worse, such as mines with a delayed explosion. When my pal and I did not rise to the bait they left us alone.

CHAPTER TWO

From Fishermen to Soldiers

THE WEEK went on with all sorts of training. Once when we were out on a night manoeuvre we blackened our faces and hands and the party I was with had to cross a small river. Well, I got to the river and heard something plumping into the water. I stopped and saw something swimming across the river and heard a sort of hissing noise. I did not know what it was so I had to get to the other side of the river and let myself sink slowly into the water. Boy, it was cold. I nearly lost my breath. Across on the other side the riverbank was very steep but there were some branches and I hauled myself up, but then all hell broke loose. There was a lot of small animals running around and jumping into the water. I found out later that they were rats.

I got away from the river and up on the railway line and I could see a man running along the track. All of a sudden he made a jump up in the air and came down flat on the railway line just for a few seconds. Then up he went and ran like the devil himself was after him. He went over to some marshes and I was only about 100 to 150 yards behind him when he disappeared. I thought he had fallen into a mineshaft or something like that so I moved forward to where I had seen him disappear. Well, I found him. He had fallen into a ditch and he could not get up. There was plenty of grass on the edges of the ditch but it was not strong enough for him to pull himself out. I called to him to find out who he was. He was one of the boys in the same platoon as me. I sat down on the side of the ditch, held on to all the grass that I could and told the boy to grab my ankles and pull himself up. After a while he came up and both of us went to our checkpoints and then back to camp.

One of the boys of the other platoon was just coming up to his checkpoint when he spotted one of the guards. This boy was not going to let the guard stop him from reporting to checkpoint, so he crept up very slowly and quietly towards him and, when he was about five feet from the guard, he jumped him. The guard did struggle. This was a thing they were told not to do if they were taken by one of the boys who were to report to checkpoint, and the same for us. If the guard caught us we had to surrender. This guard did not like to surrender so the boy from the platoon just took his tin hat off and gave the guard a few good smacks on the head.

After all the boys got through we were called into one of the lecture rooms. The old major told us that not one of the boys who were sent out to the two different checkpoints had been seen by the guards, and there was only 50 yards between each guard. But he also said that if we could not reach the checkpoint because a guard was on post, just wait and see if the guard would move. Or pick up a stone and throw it to distract the guard – not to 'clock' the guard because you might do a lot more damage than you intended. All of us agreed to that.

The training was hard but it was also a lot of fun. None of us complained about some of the rough training. We knew that it had to be hard because the training in that camp was only for a short period – just over three weeks. One of the most earth-shattering noises was when we were down in the cellar pistol range shooting at moving targets of Hitler, Goebbels and Mussolini. Those bastards just jumped up for about 30 seconds then disappeared and appeared again. We did not have earplugs so after you fired one round consisting of nine shots of a Colt 45 you could not hear very clearly for about 10 minutes.

We were out in the field practising at throwing hand grenades. One of the first grenades did not explode, so all the boys were aiming their throw where we knew the hand grenade was. But the grenade did not explode so after we were finished the armoury sergeant asked for volunteers to go and pick it up. We all wanted to go but it was only the boy who had thrown the grenade, the sergeant and another two boys that went out and brought it back. The grenade was a Mills with a 10 second fuse. What had happened was that it had not been cleaned of beeswax so the striker was stuck about halfway towards the detonator. It was dismantled and cleaned, thrown again, and then the grenade went off.

That told us that all thick grease and beeswax had to be cleaned out so that the striker would strike the detonator cap without any resistance. That could be fatal if you had to depend on your hand grenade if you were in a fight. So every man had to see that his equipment was absolutely in first class fighting order. It did save some soldiers' lives.

The unit also had to go through parachute jumping, but the boys who were taken out to man the unit's boat did not go through the training, as it was just a waste of time. Some of the boys went through a special training for mine laying along the Norwegian coast. One of my last night manoeuvres was along with eight boys, to take part in blowing up a small dummy power station, guarded by a strong guard. The demolition gang had to carry all the TNT sticks, detonators and fuses across a small river and get into the power station. All went fine until the covering party spotted a soldier who was wandering around close to where the demolition party was to enter the river. The covering unit went into action, crept up on the army person and jumped him. Six boys with planted bayonets on their rifles pointed them on the man, who started to hit back with what looked to us like a baton. The man did not say anything but he was taken away into the shelter of some trees and kept under guard.

It was a bit dark so we did not recognise the man. After that we heard the explosion and the manoeuvres were completed. We took our prisoner back to camp and took him to our lecture room, where the old major was waiting with the staff for the report from the captain from the dummy power station. When we brought the prisoner in we got a helluva big surprise. Our prisoner was the captain who was to see how the demolition job was done. But he was taken prisoner and did not see the job done. Well, I don't think it made much difference that he was taken prisoner. The job was perfect and the next day bricklayers were at the dummy station for the next unit to destroy.

On the last night manoeuvre I got a very bad cold that turned out to be bronchitis and I was put to an army hospital. There were a few New Zealanders there but mostly Welsh soldiers. I could not understand the Welsh even though one of them, who was very friendly, tried to speak to me. One of the New Zealanders said to them, "Do not try to speak your crow language to him, because when you speak to me I have to sit a long time to understand you. But when I speak to Norway very slow he understands me. Can you get that into your thick nut heads."

All the soldiers and nurses at the hospital were very nice to me. I was dismissed five days later and went back to Stoddon Park camp, where I was put up among the staff. I stayed there for seven days when the next unit arrived, and Captain Linge came and told me that I would soon be in a job.

The armoury sergeant did not want me to go, as I was the second-best rifle marksman. The best one out of 28 boys had 78 points and I had 77 points. I was very interested in guns and all sorts of firearms. I did a lot of shooting before the war.

When I had a change I left Stoddon Park camp and went back to Laleham. I was in a house where I stayed three or four days. It was a Thursday and one of the other boys and I went to a dance at Stains. We met two girls. One was in the Royal Air Force and the other worked in an office in London. They were sisters. I went for the Air Force girl whose name was Joan. My pal and I had a very enjoyable evening, so I made a date for the next evening and we went to the cinema. After that we went to a Forces club. It was very nice and the boys and girls were very friendly towards me.

On the following Sunday I met Joan and her sister and we went for a walk along the River Thames looking at the small boats and swans. It was a very enjoyable afternoon. The girls asked me many questions and if I could not answer I stopped walking and grabbed for my English dictionary to find the word to give an answer. The girls just laughed their heads off. On our walk we passed a shoe repair shop, and I said "shoe repair shop". Well, I did not pronounce my words right and the girls were laughing until the tears were streaming down their cheeks.

Joan asked me where in Norway I came from, so I took out my pocket map and found the nearest township, which was marked with a little black dot. I said without thinking, "Joan, do you see the little black prick there. That is where I come from." First it was dead silence and the girls were blushing like red traffic lights, then they started laughing. Joan said to me afterwards that was a very bad word I had used. I really should say black dot, not black prick. I never made the same mistake again.

All good things come to an end and so did my time in Stoddon Park. I had to go to London on the following Monday morning, where I was to step out of my army uniform and into navy uniform. I had three days leave and then away to Aberdeen – that was all we were told.

We arrived in Aberdeen where we were met by a leading torpedo man, a chief petty officer. He handed me some money for the trip to Lerwick. The *St. Magnus* left Aberdeen the same afternoon in a cold north-easterly. It was bitterly cold and there were no cabins, just an open fo'c'sle, not much luxury. Our food was paid for before we left Aberdeen and I believe that what we got was left-overs, but as long as we had beer with us we did not care.

The north-east wind was still blowing when we arrived in Lerwick. We got ashore and reported to our commanding officer and found out that we were navy boys and the shore staff were army. It was a puzzle just for a start until we were told the reason.

From the office we went to a small restaurant or cafe for a meal. We got egg, chips, sausages, bread and tea. After the meal we went out on the street and I met two of the boys who had been at Stoddon Park camp. One of the boys was going to Norway on a mission that same afternoon (26th October, 1941). He was one of the first boys to be shot by the bloody krauts. His name was Nils Nesse, a fine seaman.

We left Lerwick on the back of a lorry and travelled to our station at Lunna. We arrived there at teatime and met some of the other boys who had done a few trips to Norway. But as we were new and green to the station we were left to ourselves. We got to our sleeping quarters, made our beds and unpacked our kit bags. But we were not issued with a towel to dry ourselves after our bath, so we had to go to the quartermaster's and ask for towels. But he had none to give us. We were told at the navy base in Pall Mall that we would get towels when we arrived at our station. We worked a whole week and there were some very dirty jobs that we had to do. We had to use a striped cotton shirt as a towel.

It was the second Sunday that the fun started. We were ordered to start digging a road and we refused point blank. One of the sergeants, a useless old bastard, shouted, "Open revolution." Well we would show this bloody Norwegian bastard that they were in Great Britain and they could not do what they wanted. One of the old hands on the camp told the sergeant to watch what he was saying as he would get the same treatment as the captain in the Royal Air Force who called one of the skippers a bloody Norwegian quisling. That captain got a broken jaw and a broken collarbone.

We talked it over with the officer of that station and he promised that we would get what we required the next day, if we would go to work. We said we would work that day and the next day but if we did not get the items that we were short of then we would go on strike, and they could arrest us and send us back to London. On Monday afternoon at 3pm we were issued with two pillowcases and two good-sized towels. So all was OK but that good-for-nothing sergeant was transferred to some other unit or camp. We did not miss him either. After the sergeant went everything ran smoothly.

As I have mentioned already a boat called the *Siglaos* left Lerwick on the Saturday we arrived. On the way back it was attacked by a German plane and suffered a lot of damage with one man, Nils Nesse, killed. Another boat, the *Nordsjøen,* was over on a mine-laying job on the Norwegian coast and was long overdue. Nobody knew what had happened to the ship or the crew. So it was not happy days at Lunna.

It was decided that Nils Nesse was to be buried at the churchyard at Lunna, so on the funeral day the boys and most of the officers were at the base. After the funeral we sat in the recreational room at Lunna House, when we heard the familiar 'bong-bong' of a Norwegian fishing boat. Some of the old hands on the base said, "That's not the *Nordsjøen* that is coming. It must be some other refugees who have made a mistake to come into this bay, instead of going towards Lerwick." But what was strange was that the fishing boat was steaming at full speed into the harbour and went right to the *Nordsjøen's* moorings.

Nearly all of us ran down to the beach and launched rowing boats and made for the new arrival. We came alongside and we saw four bearded and dirty faces looking down at us. One of the men asked if we had a cigarette to spare so first we handed a packet to the man and then we went onboard and told them that we were new on the base.

That was my first memory of Leif Larsen, Palmer Bjørnøy, Otto Pletten and Nils Nipen. They went over with the *Nordsjøen* on the mine-laying trip and on their way back the ship sprung a leak so they had to sail into a bay near where they had just laid some mines. The ship sank to the bottom and the crew took to the small lifeboat and pulled for the shore. After some hair-raising adventures five of them eventually stole a boat called the *Arthur* and headed back for Shetland, eventually to be re-united with the skipper and engineer who had split up from the others.

The boat that just arrived at Lunna was the *Arthur.* The engine was idling while the boys sat or stood around the deck and talked, when Leif Larsen said that this was his ship and he needed an engineer and two men on deck. I went along and had a look down to the engine-room and saw that it was a 50 horse power Brunvoll engine so I told Larsen what an engine it was. He then told Palmer Bjørnøy to stop the engine and that I had to go down to the engine room and start the engine in the right rotation. As soon as the engine stopped I went down and started it. Larsen asked if I was sure that the engine ran in the right way. So I told him that all the Norwegian engines with the silencer on the port side ran to port, while the engine with the silencer on the starboard side ran to starboard. I got to be one of Leif Larsen's crew.

We had a few days with gun training and mounting a gun-stand for a double Lewis gun. That mounting had to be put in place so it would not attract too much notice, so it was placed in front of the wheelhouse near the main sail sheet fall. When I think back on that I now realise that it was bloody stupid. The mounting could have been put up forward without being in any way suspicious.

The crew of the *Arthur* had to take the boat to Lerwick to get the compass adjusted and after that was done we steamed back to Lunna. Before we came to Lunna Holm it was pitch dark with south-south-westerly wind and rain – real Shetland weather. Larsen had to ease on the speed because we could not see more than a few yards ahead of the fishing boat, but at last we arrived at Lunna Basin and went ashore up to Lunna House and had a good meal.

The following day we took the *Arthur* alongside a small pier and put onboard fuel, oil, luboil and some stores. After that she was put back to moorings. We spent the evening at Lunna House loading the pan magazines for the double Lewis gun and magazines for the Bren gun, tommy-guns and anti-tank rifle. The anti-tank rifle was our biggest gun and also the most awkward to handle. We had to put short bolts on top of the wooden railing on the bulwark to stop the gun from jumping backwards when it was fired. The man who had to use the anti-tank rifle

The author

could only fire three or four rounds if his shoulder was still intact. It was not a gun for a fishing boat, which was always pitching and rolling. Before the boat left the base each of the crew had to sign a declaration form not to tell where the boat came from, who we were working for or who we were to contact in Norway. In Norway we were not to tell where in Norway we were born or the names of our families as they might be arrested and tortured.

The men who sailed between Shetland and Norway were 'Secret Service' men. If we got caught we did not get any help from our unit, as we did not belong to anybody. We were issued with a small glass tube with poison. If we were in battle with the Germans and taken prisoner we were told 'put the glass tube in your mouth, fight to the end, and then bite the tube to release the poison'. It only took 30 seconds for the poison to finish you off. A hard decision to make, but better to be dead than to be tortured.

CHAPTER THREE

A Tough Ride from Norway

THE NEXT day it was blowing a west-north-west gale with hail showers, so it was not a time to start a trip across to Norway. The crew of the *Arthur* was Leif Larsen, Palmer Bjørnøy, Karstein Sangholt, Leif Kinn Larsen, Arne Albertsen, Otto Pletten and myself, Kaare Iversen. The crew was raring to go, especially the three new members of the crew. It was something new. Two of the new crew were brought from Norway to Shetland just a few weeks before onboard one of the unit boats. Everything went fine with no trouble, whereas I had trouble coming across. I was most anxious to get over and do some damage to the bloody Germans.

The night before we set sail for Norway some of the crew went to a dance at Vidlin Public Hall. The dance was arranged by a minister, so the good man made us welcome and wished us an enjoyable evening. It was mostly playing games, a team of girls and young married women made up the Shetland team, against the Norwegian navy team. I think it was 12 a side. Our captain was Karstein Sangholt who spoke very good English. Everything went well until the last question and that was how to spell 'Constantinople'. Karstein's opponent was a teacher, and both of them made it plain that they did not want to beat one another. They made an ass of spelling the name so to finish it was a draw. As Karstein was a foreigner he had the chance to draw matches – one long and one short. Karstein tried both matches and he found out which was the shortest one. He drew the short one that made him the loser.

The minister came over to the Norwegian navy boys and asked if we could sing a Norwegian song. We had to find out which song all the boys knew, so we came up with a song which was called "*Det var en god gammel bondemann som skulle gå ut etter øl ...*" "It was an old farmer who should go out after beer". Well the boys sang that song but that was not enough. The minister and the ladies who were working at the dance wanted us to sing another. So we did and that song had a bloody good beat to it. It was a song that we sang while marching but I was afraid that the wording would not be very nice if it was translated into English. I will say it was a bit rude, but none of the audience understood the words. They just listened to the way we sang.

We got back to Lunna House and went to bed. Next morning we got the last stores onboard the *Arthur*. We were just waiting until the afternoon so we could start the crossing over to Western Norway to Hamarset, Askrova, an isle west of Florø. We left in the afternoon of 8th November about 4pm, and the weather was in our favour. It was a west-north-west breeze, and during the night the wind faded completely away. I was on watch with Karstein Sangholt. Our watch was from 8pm until midnight. We were watching in the dark wheelhouse and talked, then Karstein asked me what sort of small handgun I had, so I told him that I had an old German Luger Pistol from 1914. Karstein told me he would give me a Colt 32 with a box of ammunition because he said the old Luger had too many faults. Of course I was glad to get a Colt 32 so I asked Karstein why he was giving it to me. In reply he told me he also had a Browning 32 and that he did not need a gun after this trip. I asked if he was to leave the *Arthur* in Norway. He said, "No, but I know that I am not coming back to base with the *Arthur*." He said that he had had a dream and in the dream he dreamt that the *Arthur* was attacked by German aircraft and that he was killed. I said to him that it was just a dream and that I didn't believe the *Arthur* was going to have an air attack. So no more was said about that.

Our trip across was not very exciting. The wind swung around to a fresh northeast and slowly increased to about 5-6 wind force. The first we saw of Norway was when it was about 50 or 60 miles away, a high mountain called Alden. We were a little to the south of where we were to land our cargo of high explosives and stuff for use in sabotage against the Germans.

The *Arthur* made land at an isle called Kinn. That was the isle where two of the crew came from so Leif Kinn got in touch with his father who came aboard and told us about the German's movements. We got some fresh fish and before we started for our destination we had a good meal. That would be our last hot meal for nearly a week. As a matter of fact it was the last meal we enjoyed together.

We started our trip towards the isles of Askrova where we had to find a place to make a dump for our cargo so our contact man could find it when he got there. To get the cargo ashore we had to use a small rowing boat but the boat could not take much – just a few boxes. First, we had to take the boxes out of the hold of the fishing boat, then over the bulwark and down to the small rowing boat, which we then rowed ashore to the beach. Then we had to take each box and carry it about 100 to 150 yards up on the isle where we made a dump.

We had 50 or 60 boxes, all of which had to be man-handled four or five times, and all the work was done in darkness. After we had all the cargo ashore it had to be covered up. We got back to the *Arthur* and made ready to put to sea. We had a cup of coffee and a sandwich as the *Arthur* was at last under way for her home base. But if we had known what was in store for us I think that we would have found a place to hide in the vessel. But we did not know what we were to run into.

I was on watch in the engine room until 8am. When I came on deck I stopped and looked towards the southeast and what I saw was not very good. It was a sort of a brass colour with stripes of red or orange. The skipper, Larsen, came and stood beside me, and pointed south-eastwards. Then he said to me, "Well what do you think of that Ivar (short for Iversen)?" I answered that if all the signs were true we were in for a hell of a storm. I went down to my bunk in the fo'c'sle and fell asleep. When I was called to take my next watch at noon I got a jug of coffee and a sandwich with bacon. I went on deck and noticed that the bulwark on the starboard side was nearly away. Just the stanchion side was left with the heavy top railings. The sea was very rough and short but big enough to do a lot of damage.

When I came off watch at 4pm I noticed that the bulwark on the portside also was a bit smashed up. It was no danger for the vessel but the sea and wind did slow the *Arthur* down and pressed her northward. The engine was working without a fault. In the late afternoon and evening the wind and sea increased in force, so sometime after midnight on the 11th November the course was altered so we got the wind and sea in over the port quarter. We were sort of running before sea and wind, with the engine at slow speed and everything onboard was a bit easy – not the sharp crack of the sea and a lot less rolling.

The sea was coming in big monstrous breakers, which came rolling as big as mountains with a white phosphorus crest. It was a terrific sight. The *Arthur* was sometimes high on top of the breakers, then down in the trough of the waves and the men in the wheelhouse could only see a grey black rushing seawall with white breakers on top. About 6.30am, *Arthur* seemed to rise on top of a great mountainous wave with the bow pointing skywards and then she seemed to be on the balance for a minute before the bow went plunging towards the bottom of the sea. It was shaking and groaning in planking and framing and the feeling I had down in the engine room was that the boat was sliding down from one shelf to another. Then the water just rushed very quickly in the engine room, with the result that the engine stopped. Next the water came from the engine room door and through the cabin bulkhead.

I made my way up to the deck. But when I came to the engine room door the boat was still submerged. The sea had free way of the deck as there was no bulwark to stop it. The men who were down in the fo'c'sle could not get out before the pressure of the sea eased off the fo'c'sle doors. The skipper was in the wheelhouse and along with him was our contact man. He had just got out of the after cabin minutes before the *Arthur* got that giant breaker. The boys from the fo'c'sle came out on deck and we took spells with the deck pump. Then somebody asked, "Where is Karstein and Arne?"

We started looking for them and we found Arne. He was hanging over the side, but there was no sign of Karstein. What saved Arne was that, when he was a young boy about 15 years old, he had broken his right elbow and the elbow was not set right so his arm had nearly a 90 degree angle. So when the sea took him his arm was acting as a hook, which went around one of the mizzen stays. If not, he would also have been lost.

We were more or less lost with the thought that Karstein was gone. We never said if somebody was lost at sea that he was dead. We just said, "He is gone west."

We got the *Arthur* pumped out and we took about 15 blankets, soaked them in diesel oil and put them over the side to dampen the breakers. The wind was so strong that the oil that came out of the blankets blew right over the vessel and landed on her lee side. I then said to skipper Larsen that we needed to rig up a sea anchor. But we had nothing we could use. The only thing we had was a big box where the anchor chain was coiled down, so one of the other men and I started to hand the anchor chain out onto the deck. When the box was empty we took some rope and made a double sling around the box, then we shackled a heavy mooring rope to the double sling and dumped the lot over the side. We paid out all of the rope that we had. It was about 30 or 40 fathoms long. The so-called anchor did work well. The *Arthur* swung a little and took the sea fine.

I finished on deck and went down to give the engineer a hand to clean out the crankcase of the engine from the seawater. As long as we were working then *Arthur* was fine. The engineer started the engine about 3pm and it was not long after that the mooring rope to the sea anchor broke. It was a giant of a breaker that did it. So now we had to steam very slowly against the wind.

It was dangerous to be out on deck as the sea was washing over it all the time so the only place the crew could use was the wheelhouse and the engine room. It was always two men in the wheelhouse, one man in the chartroom, and four men in the engine room. Arne seemed to be in a sort a coma but we could not do much for him. We got him laid down in the engine room so there was not much room to move about. Then the question arose about something to eat. The galley was out of the question as the doors had been smashed in and what foodstuff we had there was soaked in seawater. But we had bread, butter, tins of cooked bacon and tinned beans in the cabin forward, but no place to get food warmed up.

It was decided that one man had to go forward to the fo'c'sle to bring some food to the engine room, so skipper Larsen said I was to do it. I went and got a couple of loaves, a tin of butter and some tins of beans and bacon, a big kettle of cold water and seven jugs. I made two trips over the deck. On the first trip I found a rope, made it secure near the engine room door, brought it forward to the anchor winch, tightened it as well as I could and made it fast.

I found my cigarette ration of about 240 and matches and brought that up to the engine room. So now we had food and cigarettes. We were all soaking wet. We did not notice that before, but there was nothing we could do about it. We just had to let our clothes dry on our bodies.

This was now the second day out from Norway. It was Tuesday, 11th November, and the weather was just the same. As I have said before the space we had to use was next to nothing. Arne was lying between the engine and starboard fuel tank. He had an oilskin coat over his reefer jacket, but he could not avoid touching the flywheel with his right arm. The result was that the flywheel ground a hole right through his oilskin, reefer and tunic, right onto his arm. It was his cousin Leif L. Kinn who came down from the wheelhouse and took a look at him. He noticed that Arne's arm was rubbing against the flywheel. He got help from one of the crew and managed to move Arne away from the flywheel to a more secure place.

During the night the *Arthur* got a good many breakers over the deck, but as there was no bulwark left on either side the sea had free passage over the deck. The Brunvoll engine was running with a steady 'bong bong', a very assuring sound, but the crew was all wondering how long the storm would last.

They were also thinking and wondering about the *Blia*, which was also out on a trip to a place near Bergen. She was a well boat and she had a hatch for loading live fish. We were hoping that the *Blia* was still somewhere along the Norwegian coast as we thought that with such a big loading hatch and powerful engine she would not withstand such a storm and such big breakers. Sometimes from the wheelhouse of the *Arthur*, when the ship was on top of a wave crest, we could see breakers 100 to 150 yards long. It was a very hard strain on the nerves of the men. If just a part of the wave hit the vessel there would be nothing left – perhaps just a few broken planks.

The first night after we were broken down passed slowly and Wednesday, 12th November was just like the Tuesday, no moderating of the storm and the breakers just the same. The food we had brought to the engine room was nearly finished. There was not a drop of water left, so I went to the fo'c'sle to bring up some more water and other food stuff – tins of cold baked beans, corned beef and tins of cooked bacon. After all that was brought to the engine room, we had to put the food into iron buckets and hang them up above the engine as that was the only place. But the bread dried up and the tins of bacon and beans, which were open, got a strong taste of diesel oil. Some of the crew could not keep the food down, so it had to come up and whoever felt sick went up the ladder to the engine room door and delivered the food over the deck. The sea just washed the stuff away so there was always a clean deck.

I was always thinking about how we could get into the after cabin. It was just a wooden bulkhead between the engine room and the cabin, but we had no tools to cut the planks in the bulkhead. The only thing I had was a good sharp knife and I thought that I could manage to cut the planks with it. So I started with the knife and hammer. It was a slow progress but after about three hours I had cut four planks and managed to get into the cabin. I had to shift a chest of drawers, and when that was done we could get in without too much struggle. That gave us two more bunks to sleep in although the blankets were soaking wet.

We had some blankets left in the fo'c'sle and I went forward and brought them up. After we got them three men went into the cabin. Arne got a bunk for himself and the rest of the crew shared the other bunk. We tried the wireless – but that was no use. The set was destroyed with seawater. Next we checked the barometer. Just plink on the glass and 'by Jove' the barometer needle went up a few points. We thought the storm was soon to be over as the barometer was rising. So whenever a man came into the cabin he had a plink at the barometer and up it went. But the storm was just the same.

By Thursday, 13th November, we had been at sea from Monday the 10th, and the weather was not moderating at all. On Wednesday we heard a hell of a bang. When we went out on deck to look at what it was we found that the mast had fallen down on the stern. Well, Leif and I made the mast secure until daylight. When we got enough light that we could see why the mast had fallen down, we found that the rigging screws on the forward stays had stripped their thread. The mast was still secure, so there was no more that we could do about it.

About 1.30pm we heard a sharp crack, and one of the men from the wheelhouse came sliding down the ladder from the chart room. He said that a plane was over us. I took a Bren gun and went out on deck, but I did not fire at the plane, which I recognised as a Messer Schmitt 110. He made another turn around us but did not fire again. He likely thought that we were finished so he would not waste ammo on such a wreck.

We believed that we were nearer the Norwegian coast than Shetland, so the next thing we started to think about was how much fuel oil we had left. We had no chance to sound the fuel tanks from the deck, but as we had just steamed with a quarter to half speed, we were sure that we had enough fuel. Our spare drum of diesel oil was used the first morning after we had the big breaker, so we could not do a thing about it.

The day passed away and with the darkness the wind rose quite a bit. About midnight the ship got a big breaker on the port bow that swung the ship to starboard before the men at the wheel could swing the *Arthur* up against the sea. We got one right amidships with the result that the wheelhouse was pushed a good piece over and one wheelhouse door burst inwards while the other went outwards. The middle window was half open and stuck there; it could not go up or down. Now it was a job to fix the doors and we were lucky we found two bundles of fish box material in a locker in the after cabin. After we had patched up the doors, we put boxwood between the stays of the wheelhouse and the doors. It was two stays on either side of the doors, and that made a good secure hold for the wood that stood until we got the doors fixed at Lunna. The rest of the night went on without any more excitement. Friday, 14th November was still a howling gale but the sea was a little better. The rain was not so heavy but we could not see more than about 100 yards.

We got more bread and water from the fo'c'sle. Larsen asked if the big roast we got from the cook when we left was still there. So I went to the galley and had a look around. Yes, I found the pot with the roast. The pot was full of seawater. The roast had been ready to eat when we left Lunna. I took the pot, poured the sea water out and brought it down to the engine room. Larsen came down and when he saw the big roast, he said, "Well I am fed up with cold beans and bacon, so I will have roast, cold water and dry bread." The roast was a bit tough so the knives we had were no use. Larsen took his knife and sliced off enough of the steak so that there was enough for the crew. The side of steak, which was lying at the bottom of the pot, had got rusted, so each man had to tear that piece off. But, 'by Jove', it was very tasty. It was likely the best that we had had for a whole week. The last warm meal we had had was on Monday, 10th November.

We still had no idea where we were. Were we near the Norwegian coast or were we nearer Shetland than we believed? We had no way to find out, so we just had to wait until next morning. On Saturday, 15th November it was still a gale but it moderated a bit. The rain had stopped and the sea had gone down, so when the daylight came we decided to take a chance to sound the fuel tanks. I went out on deck and signalled to Larsen to swing the *Arthur* so we could run afore the wind and sea. I got a sounding and that was just a shock. We had just about nine inches of fuel in the starboard tank. That was about 200 litres. So all told we had about 300 litres of fuel. That was only enough to steam for about 18 or 20 hours.

When I got up to the wheelhouse and told Larsen, he did not know what to say. We had 18 to 20 hours steaming time, and we were hoping that we could see land – either Shetland or Norway – but the hope was that we could see Shetland. We got the log clock and checked the mileage and found out that we had steamed a distance of 110 miles. That was where we got the big breaker on Tuesday morning, so we came to the conclusion that we had passed Shetland and were on the west side.

We needed more bread and water and I was the fellow who had the job to bring the food up. I went forward and got what was needed and handed the food and water down to the engine room. I then went to the galley to see if I could get the stove to work, but no luck. The pipe was broken just about the galley deck head. I then stood in the galley door and looked to the west. The *Arthur* was steaming against the wind and sea, I just stood there and then I saw something like a black wall. I stood there for a while then I knew where we were.

I went to the wheelhouse and said to Larsen, "I know where we are.

We are about half a mile from Fetlar, so we can steam south-west and we will soon be at Lunna Bay." Larsen did not believe me so he swung the *Arthur* around and steamed along the coastline. Larsen asked me, "How in hell can you say that the land we saw was Fetlar?" I told him that the black rock face was the first sight I had of Shetland and that I would not have made a mistake about that. I also told Larsen that off the north end of the isle was a holm with a very narrow sound. When we came abreast of that part then Larsen said, "Yes, Ivar, you are right," We steamed towards Lunna Bay, and it was a sorry sight that met us. Three boats that had been lying at anchor had drifted ashore and were high and dry on the beach.

The *Arthur* was taken to her mooring and some rowing boats came from the shore to welcome us back. We then asked about the *Blia* but there was no word about her. We were hoping that she was still in Norway, but we got word afterwards that she had left Norway with 43 passengers and crew onboard. We knew then that she had 'gone west', that was the slogan we used if we lost a crew member or ship.

We went ashore but we could not walk properly. We had got the motion of a rolling deck so instead of walking we were staggering like a lot of drunk men. We got to our room and found clean clothing and went for a bath. We had to take the bath in turns because there was only one bath tub. Arne asked our head officers why they did not send a ship or plane to look for us. We got the answer that the ship went down and the plane crashed and cars and lorries were blown off the road. Arne did not see why the officer included cars and lorries for a rescue out at sea in a hurricane.

At last all of us had had a bath and a good meal, but we could not eat much as we were thinking about our crew member who was lost, and our seven friends onboard the *Blia*. It was only about three weeks since the first crewman was shot onboard the *Siglaos*. There was a depressing feeling at the base. The quarter-master went to Lerwick to get a couple of bottles of whisky. But no luck. He only got a half bottle of brandy and a bottle of champagne. When he came back to the base the whole crew of the *Arthur* was invited to his room for a drink. He opened the bottle of champagne and poured seven glasses. Some of the men could not stand more than a glass and a half and they just dropped off to sleep. In a way it was no wonder since there was none of the crew who had had a right sleep since the Sunday and it was now Saturday – a whole week without proper food or sleep. It took quite a bit before we were okay again.

CHAPTER FOUR

Sailings Become Routine

AFTER BREAKFAST on Sunday, 16th November we went onboard the *Arthur*. The first thing I did was to sound the fuel tank and I really got a shock. The sounding on the starboard tank was only six inches and the port tank only four inches. The total fuel was less than 75 litres all told. When I sounded the tanks the ship was rolling so I had got a wrong reading. But never mind. We had made it back to base.

The crew started to clean up in the after cabin and also the fo'c'sle. We had to bring all the guns ashore for cleaning but we could not find the double Lewis gun. We found only one but the rest had gone overboard when we got the big breaker. Guns and ammunition were brought ashore and were cleaned by shore staff.

On Monday, 17th November the crew got new rigging screws and got the after mast set again. Now came the job of repairing the bulwarks. We had no proper wood for that job. The planks were not dressed but no-one would notice that after we had painted them. When we painted the bulwarks white, the paint looked dirty and that suited us fine. It was no good to have a well-painted boat in Norway at that time. When the mast was up again and the bulwarks were nearly the same as before, it was time to take the ship alongside the quay to refuel. On Tuesday, 18th November we brought the *Arthur* alongside the quay and started refuelling with gasoil. We also got two drums of lubricating oil, filled the fresh water tanks and checked stores. A carpenter from the base repaired the galley doors so that she was once more ship-shape.

We asked if it was possible for us to get a drift sea anchor made as we had found out that it was a good thing to have in case we got caught with such a storm as we had just had. Well we got the sea anchor and a heavy manilla rope. The sea anchor came to the ship, but the frame was not put together. It was very difficult to transport on a lorry along with all other sorts of items, but nevertheless we got the whole lot onboard, put it together and lashed it alongside the port-side of the engine room casing. The rope was coiled down in a big box where the anchor cable box had been. The anchor cable was stored down in the hold in another cable box. The wheelhouse doors were also repaired and so was the centre window, so now the *Arthur* was ready for another trip.

We did not have to wait long for another trip, but we could not leave because the weather was nearly as bad as ever. At last we got a sort of a moderate weather forecast from the RAF that the wind was going round to west-north-west moderate. The *Arthur* started on the second trip on Monday, 24th November. We left the base about 4pm. When we came clear of Out Skerries we got a fresh wind from the south. It was nearly gale force but we kept a steady course eastward. The wind did not swing to west-north-west but was steady southerly and slightly increasing and there was a heavy sea running from the south-east with big breakers, so we had to slow down to about half speed.

About 10am on Tuesday, 25th November the sea was so bad that Larsen and crew decided to drop the sea anchor and drift with that until the weather moderated. Olaf Kinn and I unleashed the sea anchor and made ready to drop over the side, when we noticed the sea was very calm a few hundred yards away from us so we steamed forward to it. Just before we came to the calm part of the sea the wind dropped to barely a light breeze, so we did not have to use the drift anchor. We kept steaming eastward and sighted land about 4pm. We reckoned that we were about 35 to 40 miles from land.

At 8pm it had started to blow from the south-south-east and it started to rain so the visibility was not very good. At 8.30pm we spotted an island and a lot of breakers. We had got into shallow water and did not know where we were so we turned back and steamed out on a westerly course for two hours. We slowed down and hove to, then the engine stopped. We discovered that we had got water in the fuel oil, so we drained off the water until we got clean fuel and started up again. There was no more trouble with the engine.

At 7am we swung around to a north-easterly course and steamed away for about two and a half hours when we saw a lighthouse. We recognised which one it was. It was the Ytterøy lighthouse. We had made land too far to the south, and now it was blowing a strong south-south-west gale. We just kept going until we came to the isles of Bueland and that was not far from our destination. We steamed through a sound and came to a big holm with a quay where we moored up.

We were in full uniform when we came alongside the quay. The people on the mainland thought we were Germans, so they did not come to the isle to investigate – not before it was dark. There were three men who came but they did not come on board. They just walked on the quay. One of the crew went to the galley to make coffee and once they smelled the coffee they came onboard and started to speak. They were invited down in the fo'c'sle for a cup of coffee and white bread. The men never asked where we came from or what we were doing there. We were stormbound there for two days and in the late afternoon we had quite a few visitors onboard. We made coffee and cocoa and got quite a lot of information about the Germans.

On the third day we steamed towards the place where we had one man with a radio transmitter and a small generator. After we finished the job we steamed away into a narrow sound to await darkness. We went ashore and were standing on the bank looking at the *Arthur* and speaking about what a good boat she was when we got a shock. We noticed that we had two different registration numbers. On one side the number was M 190 B, the other side was H 190 B. The first number was for the county surrounding Ålesund, while the other was for the county around Bergen. The two places were about 200 miles apart. Just before we had left Lunna base we had altered the registration numbers from M 190 B to H 190 B. The M was made into an H but the paint we had used was not really dry enough so when we got out to sea the spray washed off the paint. There was nothing we could do about it because we did not have any white paint onboard to paint a new H. About 5pm we started on the trip back. It was just a south-south-west moderate breeze and we arrived in Lunna in good spirit.

It was then decided to get another boat, a lot bigger than *Arthur*, as she had to have a full refit at Scalloway. So we steamed to another bay where a boat was moored and Larsen and crew got the 75-foot *Feie*. The *Arthur* and the *Feie* steamed from the bay at Catfirth to Lerwick and the *Feie* was moored alongside the breakwater in Victoria dock. The following day Larsen, Otto Pletten and I took the *Arthur* around Sumburgh Head to Scalloway where she was for about two months, being put into seaworthy order again. The *Feie's* engine had to have a full overhaul and it took about one month before we were able to start it.

Before Christmas we noticed a Norwegian fishing boat in Lerwick Harbour but we did not speak to any of the crew of this boat. They were in Lerwick for only a couple of days. At Christmas there was a party for the Norwegian crew and some of the others. It was in the Masonic Hall and a Norwegian army Captain was present. We all knew him as we had met him in London and also at our training camps. He was a great man, a person you could really respect and trust, in other words he was a friend and one of the boys. Little did we know that he was going on a raid in Måløy where he was to be killed by a German. The unit lost one of its best-liked and respected men.

We were all very sorry at the loss, but we could not stop now. Instead we all put our minds to try to get revenge for Captain Linge. The men of the unit did a lot of damage to the Germans – not really because of Captain Linge, but because the Germans were such arrogant bastards, and they used all sorts of excuses to show the Norwegians that they had the power to do what they wanted, along with the most hated quislings. The story of Captain Linge's death was written in another book, so I will not go any further into that story.

Christmas celebrations over, we started work on the *Feie* to get the engine ready for trips to Norway in the new year. On New Year's Eve all the gates to the harbour were closed about 8am and the boys of the *Feie* were ashore at the canteens for a good few beers. When we came down to Victoria Pier the gate was closed and we could not get into the dock or get to the *Feie*. As it was New Year's Eve there was a lot of people around so we asked some if they could help us to move the double gates so we could get to our ship.

Well, we got plenty of boys to help us, so we lifted the double gates off the hinges and pulled them right over to the lifeboat shed and left them there. We asked the Lerwick boys if they would come onboard for a beer but they refused the invitation. We got onboard the *Feie* and had some beer and then we started the engine. Yes, that was a great moment when the engine started without any trouble. We let the engine idle for nearly three hours.

New Year's Day was a fine day so the boys on the *Feie* and the *Aksel*, which had also had a big overhaul to the engine, decided to take them for a trial run. The two ships left the Victoria dock and started running from the south end of the harbour up to the north end. We may have done a couple of trips each way, when we noticed someone at the Malakoff signalling with a flag. So we went alongside and asked what was up. One of our officers told us that the Forces in Lerwick were put on alert because they noticed the two boats come steaming at full speed from the south entrance of the harbour. They thought it was two boats with Germans to draw the attention away from other places south of Lerwick.

Well, we got a bloody good telling off for taking the boat out into the harbour without permission from our officers and also from the Royal Navy commander. We had only one thing to say, that was that we had to have a trial run, and since there were no other boats or ships moored in the harbour we had the full length to run, and if we had found any fault we would have steamed to Victoria dock. We steamed from the Malakoff to Victoria dock and moored both ships alongside each other. No more was said about the incident.

We were still working on the *Feie* to make her so we could go from the cabin through the engine room and into the cargo hold. The *Feie* had two fuel tanks on each side of the engine room, but they were too small. They could only hold about 800 kilos of gasoil, so we had to carry barrels in the cargo hold and pump the fuel with a big pump into each tank. We were thinking of the trip with the *Arthur* so we were going to have a good supply of fuel onboard.

We were working on the *Feie* and got a sea anchor onboard all ready and lashed that alongside the wheelhouse port side. We got a steel access made, leading from the deck to the engine room. We also got 120 fathoms manilla rope, three inches thick, for the sea anchor. When in Lerwick we got both fuel tanks filled up and took on barrels of luboil. In the hold we loaded twenty 40-gallon barrels of gasoil, and fresh water, so now we were ready to take a trip to Norway when the chance came. We left Lerwick for Lunna, and the trip went without any trouble.

While lying at Lunna we had an accident in the after cabin. We had a double primus cooker and one of the crew was making tea, when the primus exploded and it started to burn on the bulkhead. We got the fire out but the paint on the deckhead and the varnished bulkhead was scorched badly. We had to scrape the deckhead and the bulkhead, then paint and varnish. The crewman got some burn blisters on his hands so he had to attend the doctor, but after three or four days he was OK.

Also when lying at Lunna we got an order to go to Whalsay to escort a Norwegian fishing boat which had arrived there late on that evening. We had to take another ship. She was the biggest one we had, an iron ship called *Erkna*. There were four of us who went; I as an engineer, Larsen as skipper, Alveberg and Petersen as crew. Well the trip went OK.

We arrived at Whalsay and saw the Norwegian fishing boat. She was the *Heland* and she had come over with one of Linge's men onboard. The Linge man had to get out of Norway as the German Gestapo was after him.

The man, Karl Johan Aarsæther contacted the skipper of the *Heland* and asked if he could make a trip to Shetland. The *Heland* was engaged in winter fishing on the west coast of Norway so she was away for a few days from her home port and was able to make the trip. We escorted the *Heland* to Lunna, where she got fuel. She could carry 10 tonnes of fuel in two tanks, so if she had to get away in a hurry she had enough fuel onboard to take her back to Shetland. Well, about three weeks later she had to take the final trip to Shetland as the Gestapo was after her skipper and crew. Skipper Sevrin Roald brought his wife over with him, and after a trip to London, he, his wife and his brother came back to Shetland, joining the unit.

The crew of the *Feie* was asking if there was a chance to take a trip over to Norway and we got the opportunity to go north to Kristiansund where we would have to steam into a long narrow fjord to land our radio operator. The *Feie* left Lunna on the 23rd January, 1942 and steamed on a course for the Stad area. About 2am the engine overheated on the forward main bearing so we had to stop and pump luboil into the bearing. The wind was a light south-west so we had the mizzen sail up. All of a sudden the wind changed from the south-west to a north-west gale with the result that the mizzen boom broke. There were only five men on deck, so the skipper tried to swing the *Feie* off the wind but to no avail. The sail was flapping about with the end of the boom, and Leif Kinn and myself tried to get the mizzen sail down. But something had gone wrong with the running, so the sail came only half way down the mast and was flapping and throwing the end of the mizzen boom.

Leif and I got hold of the bottom of the sail and pulled. All of a sudden the sail came down, but it was still not secured and the piece of the boom was still being thrown about. Leif got a glancing blow and went down on deck. The next I knew was that I had a hell of a pain in my left side and my back. Leif said to me that he had been hurt on his right side, but we would have to lift some rope to lash the sail. I think the operation took us about half an hour, but we could not use the mizzen without a mizzen boom.

The engineer, Bjørnøy had got the engine started and we began to steam towards the Stad area. The wind stayed south-easterly in the morning and freshened to gale force about nine, and very cold. Every drop of seawater froze as soon as it came onboard. In the afternoon we discovered that the *Feie* was taking water somewhere forward so we had to use the emergency pumps. But the leakage was not serious so the pump was shut off when we came near the coast and the sea was nearly smooth.

The *Feie* steamed along the coast, and we got a message on the wireless that the area we had come through was out of bounds and all shipping was to stop for German patrol boats. We went into a bay north of Måløy hoping to get better information about this last checking of the coastal traffic. We found out that all boats which were passing Måløy, and as far north as Kristiansund, had to stop for inspection by the Germans, so we decided to go south and get another boat instead of the *Feie*.

On the last trip with the *Arthur* we had landed a wireless operator. The place he was at was just in our course, so we decided to call along and find out how he was getting on. As soon as we came alongside the quay the man came onboard and asked if we had come to take him back to Britain. He had been there over two months and his transmitter set had not worked for most of the time he was there. The fellow we had with us asked to get the transmitter onboard to test the set from the *Feie*. It was brought onboard along with its generating set. We put the generator down in the hold, put a rubber hose from the exhaust pipe and started up. The engine got too hot with the long exhaust pipe so we took it off and let it go out in the hold. No-one thought about the exhaust gases which were more or less trapped in the hold, as we found out later.

When we were lying alongside the quay we decided to top up our fuel tanks from barrels in the hold. We had a fairly big rotary pump in the hold and plenty of two and a half inch rubber hose. We started to pump fuel oil about 6.30am and when this was going on two of the crew went to another fishing place to see if they could find another fishing boat, better than the *Feie*, but they had no luck. They returned to the *Feie* and when they came onboard they saw some of the crew running and throwing themselves down on the snow on the quay. Then they noticed that one of the crew was lying on the deck, and the wireless operator was giving him artificial respiration. That man was one of the men who had worked with me for little over an hour.

I felt a terrible headache so I went to the fo'c'sle and turned in. I had told the man who took over the pumping that I was going to lie down. He pumped away until he also felt a headache so he went to the fo'c'sle to call me. He did not get any answer so he raised the alarm. When the rest of the crew came on deck they also felt sort of sick. They got me up on deck and started to bring me back, and I did come around. I noticed that I was lying on deck on top of a blanket just in my underwear. I was freezing and my back was in very bad pain. I asked for a cigarette and got the answer that I had had enough smoke for a while. They took away all my cigarettes and my matches.

We did not get contact with London, so we decided to return to Shetland with both the wireless operators. We had to move from the quay so we steamed to a bay where nobody would see us. It was no good to go to sea as it was early morning and no fishing boat went to sea at that time. We went into the bay and dropped anchor, had our breakfast and then started to clean our guns. In the afternoon a rowing boat with two men came alongside and told us that a German patrol boat was out on the other side of the isles, exploding drift mines. We could not do anything but stay put, as it would soon be dark. We were ready if the Germans came into the bay, but luckily for us the German patrol boat passed just about half a mile from the entrance. As soon as it was dark we started up and started our return trip to Shetland.

The trip back to Shetland did not go without some trouble. All went fine until in the afternoon when we spotted the radio mast at Haroldswick. We estimated that we were about 30 to 35 miles off. Then the engine started to overheat and before we could do anything about it, the top of the engine cracked and the cooling water gushed out through the crack.

We stopped the engine, dismantled the cooling water pump and found that one of the valves was jammed. We got that fixed then started to look at what emergency repair we had to do to stop the cooling water running down the engine. We made a heavy wooden frame which fitted around the top of the cylinder head where the crack was, and from the four corners of the frame we put wooden stanchions up under the wheelhouse deck and some wooden wedges in under the stanchion to press the crack together.

While this work was being done in the engine room the deck crew was busy getting the sails rigged so the *Feie* could get steering speed. We got under way with the sail, and the engine again started but the crack was not completely closed up. Quite a lot of cooling water got into the engine room. To make matters more awkward the water channel underneath the engine had blocked up so most of the cooling water ran down in the bilges in the fore end of the engine room and under the big flywheel where it was thrown around.

The only thing we could do to stop the water from reaching the flywheel was to use a two pound jam tin as a scoop in the opening between the flywheel and the ship's timber. We used three buckets and when one bucket was filled it was handed man to man and emptied on the deck. The tin was just a little bit too big but we did not have anything else. We kept going like that for six or seven hours until we arrived at Lunna. Yes we were really worn out after that trip.

After a couple of days we started to dismantle the top of the engine to bring down to Scalloway for repairs. By that time there were three

Norwegian engineers working at William Moore's engineering shop. I was working for only one day with sort of heavy work but my back was so sore that I got light work to clean guns and also empty the gun magazines we had had on the trip.

Base staff and staff of Messrs Wm Moore and Sons Workshop.

After a few days we got our old boat back, the *Arthur*, as we had an important trip to do and the *Arthur* was the only boat in the base at the time. So the *Arthur* was made ready for the trip and we got the cargo loaded and provisions onboard. We sailed in the afternoon of the 8th of February, 1942 on a course for an isle outside Trondheim Fjord. We had two wireless operators onboard so we had to land at a convenient place with a chance for further transport into Trondheim.

The trip went well with no unusual happenings. We got land and steamed towards our destination, and then it started snowing. The wind had been very moderate but now it was blowing a gale from the north-west and the visibility was not very good. To make matters worse the engine slowed down to just over half speed. We got alongside a quay and stopped the engine and found the fault right away. It was a bolt in the governor's system that had got loose and unscrewed, so the governor was only half working. Bjørnøy and I dismantled the governor and were nearly finished when skipper Larsen came and told me to come up on deck because a ship was steaming towards us and using its search-light on us. I got the biggest gun, an anti-tank rifle. I got the gun into position and was ready. I had to aim below the portholes in the engine room, while the rest of the crew would use Bren guns and tommy guns on the wheelhouse and other deckhouses. The ship was only 30-40 metres from us and we were ready to open up on it when we heard the klap, klap on the quay and a man came onboard and told us for God's sake do not shoot at the ship. It was the doctor's transport for going to outlying isles.

Well, we put the guns away and then the thought came to us that it was a very close shave for the doctor and his crew. It would also likely have been curtains for us too as we were very near a German coastal post with one or two patrol boats.

I went back to the engine room and helped Bjørnøy to finish off the job. We then started the engine to make sure it was okay. Then we stopped the engine and cleaned up, had a meal then turned in for the night's sleep without being tossed about in the bunk. Three of the deck crew divided the night watch between them, four hours each man.

Next morning we found out that a mail boat was calling at another fishing village. That was the earliest chance for the two men we had onboard to go into Trondheim Fjord, bringing with them their gear and also the cargo we had onboard. That included six herring barrels containing twelve 27-pound time-set mines, six or eight empty beer bottle cases with double bottoms and in the double bottoms were packed six Luger pistols with ammunition. We also had some paint drums, also double, and they contained high explosives. The mines had a clock timer and after so many minutes or hours, the mine would explode. The 12 mines were laid in the harbour, and they gave the Germans a bad time as they did not know what was going on, as they could not find any trace after each explosion.

The *Arthur* steamed at half speed and the two men who were to go ashore each had a big scrap book and pretended to make drawings of the voe and the surrounding isles and hills. They also had a chart about the area lying on the main hatch, which they consulted now and again.

We went alongside the innermost quay where there were a few fishermen. One of the men we had onboard asked if it was here that the mailboat stopped, and he was told that it was the other quay. He also asked about the tidal stream in the area, and the fisherman told him that if the tidal stream was right it was possible that there would be plenty of work there.

The *Arthur* then steamed the short distance to the other quay where we discharged the cargo and the two men went ashore. Before we left we were told that the mailboat would be there about noon. At Svellingen we saw a few German soldiers. When we steamed out past the lookout post about 50 or 60 metres away, up on a hillock, the German soldier on watch gave us a wave with his arm. We responded and steamed away, running in among some isles where we dropped the anchor to await darkness.

I was not feeling too good. My back was giving me pure hell especially when I was lying in my bunk, turning and tossing from side to side. At 5pm we were under way for Shetland and we got a good push along by a north-north-east gale during the afternoon watch from 12 to 4. The sea was very rough and the *Arthur* was steaming at full speed before the sea. As she ran away on the crest of a big breaker, suddenly there was no water under the bow, and she fell like a stone. Although shaking very badly, she never stopped but just ran into the next breaker. By then we had slowed down to half speed.

I was on watch when I noticed that she was making water, so I started the deckwash pump to check how much water had come in. I told the skipper what was happening so we kept the deckwash pump on. We knew then she had got a fairly bad leak somewhere but we could not investigate at that time. This was our second ship that had sprung a leak so we wondered what would be the next to happen to us.

The weather moderated until we had a light breeze and we arrived at Lunna basin on the 14th of February, put the *Arthur* to her mooring and went ashore about 3pm. The whole crew was more or less worn out. We had a bath, a shave and a good meal and then we were not too bad.

When the boats were out on trips no-one was allowed to wash as the fresh water capacity was not sufficient to use for washing. There was also the fear that the ship might be attacked by aircraft and shelled and the water tanks holed. When the crew got their rooms issued, they felt pretty good and soon went to bed. All except me. My back was as bad as ever and I made up my mind to see a doctor.

The following morning when we got up it was still dark. After breakfast, when it was light enough to see Lunna harbour and the *Arthur*, we noticed that she was low in the water. When the crew got onboard we found that the boat was half full of water. Some of the crew manned the big deck pump and started pumping. Three of the crew went to another boat and started up and went alongside the *Arthur*. They put a hose onboard and started pumping with a strong wheel pump and after about three hours the vessel was dry. Now the engine had to be cleaned out and when that was done the engine was started and run at idling speed with the deckwash pumps running to keep the ship empty. The *Arthur* was then taken alongside the quay at Lunna and all the bedding was brought ashore as it was soaking wet.

Next day the boat steamed to Lerwick to go on the slipway to be repaired. The damage showed that the fastener of the planking on the starboard side had been drawn when the vessel fell on the sea. The carpenter at the slip put 178 through bolts in the starboard side forward and afterwards she was caulked and painted.

With the *Arthur* on the slip and the *Feie* still out of commission, the crew did not have much to do. I went to see the doctor as my back still gave me a lot of pain. I was taken to Lerwick, where I went to a civilian doctor. He asked me what had happened, and I told him. The doctor then sort of examined my back. When he put a slight pressure on the small of my back it was sore. The doctor did not think it was anything serious – just a slight disorder of the kidneys. He sounded my chest and told me that I had a bad cold and then told me to go to the naval hospital in Lerwick. I was advised not to tell the hospital staff that I had seen a civilian doctor.

When I got to the hospital I wasn't examined but I got a bed. In the afternoon my temperature was taken and marked down on a card. No other examination was done and my temperature was not taken again. I was in the naval hospital for nine days. I was not examined by any doctors and I did not get any medicine either. All the fellows who were in the so-called hospital were called about 6.30am and given a cup of tea. After that we had to make our beds and sweep the floors. Next we went for a shave and a wash and waited for breakfast. When that was over we had to wait for the doctor. We had to stand at attention at the foot of our beds when the doctor came around. He picked up your card and had a quick glance at it and then passed on to the next man. Sometimes the doctor asked, "Are you okay?" The answer was mostly, "Yes sir."

Well, I did not think much of the medical side of the hospital, I never got anything for my cold or for the pain in my back. On the ninth day I was in hospital I asked if I could go out, and that was granted but I was not to go before the canteen was closed. I got out of the hospital and made my way down the main street where I met some of our boys from some of the other boats.

One of the boats lying at Victoria dock was the *Askel*. That was not far from Kay's grocery shop so I went there and got a bottle of rum. I got the rum and beer onboard the *Askel* and the crew and I had a good afternoon. We went ashore to Henry's cafe and had our tea and after that we went to the canteen on the Hillhead and stayed there. When the canteen was closed we went onboard the *Askel* and had a drink before I went back to the hospital. I got in there about 12.30am and when I asked the sick bay attendant if he wanted my uniform he told me that I had to leave next morning before breakfast. I did so but I did not see the doctor before I walked out.

I went down to our office and reported that I was out of the so-called navy hospital. I then went down to the harbour and went onboard the *Askel* where I had a cup of coffee. After that I went to a chemist shop and got some cough mixture then got transport out to Lunna. I took my cough mixture and it was not long before I was clear of the cold, but my back still hurt like hell.

During the time I was in hospital the *Feie* had been put into commission again and she had been on a trip for about 40 hours. She left to go across to Norway but after about 14 hours at sea the skylight over the fo'c'sle was lifted off the coaming and the fo'c'sle was more or less flooded. The crew had not secured the skylight before they went to sea, so they had to return to base. But that was not the only trouble. The ship had a bad leak forward somewhere so the *Feie* was moored up.

Once more the crew of the *Arthur* and the *Feie* got another boat. She was the *Feiøy*, slightly smaller than the *Feie*. I did not like the look of the side of the ship as she had been ashore three times on a rocky beach, and the false keel was lying on the beach. What we could see of the side of the bilges at the bow was not a good sight. The side was badly scoured and I thought there would be a lot more damage along the keel and the bottom.

We got orders to take the ship alongside the quay to load the cargo and also to take onboard food, water, etc. We loaded about 10 or 15 tonnes of high explosives. This cargo was to be discharged on an isle outside of Bergen. But before we were ready to leave, we were told that one of the other boats had been over to the Norwegian coast, very near the place that we were to go to. There were about 200 or 300 German soldiers there. The whole area was declared out of bounds and any fishing boat or other craft would undergo a thorough search. Our trip was cancelled.

Instead we were ordered to take the cargo to a place south of Bodø in the north of Norway, a sailing distance of about 600 miles, with a ship which I reckoned was not seaworthy. And I said so. "I will not refuse to sail on any of the boats we have here, provided they are seaworthy and safe. But I refuse to sail on the *Feiøy* in the state she is in now. I am not stopping any of the other men from sailing but common sense tells me that the ship is more or less a coffin as she is now. I suggest we discharge the cargo and when the *Arthur* is off the slip we put the *Feiøy* on the slip. And I can tell you that you will get a hell of a surprise to see the state of the keel planks and the rest of the bottom of the ship. All the other boys and myself have volunteered to do the job as it is put to us, but not to take a boat which is not seaworthy. That is just plain suicide and dead sailors are for no use."

The skipper Larsen called a meeting in our sleeping quarters, and he started accusing Viken, one of the crew, saying that the man was after the skipper's job. Viken told Larsen that he did not want to go on the previous trip, but he did so as the *Arthur* was short of one man. He said he preferred to work ashore, and he told Larsen to remove his name from the crew's list.

Larsen then asked me if I would go on the trip with the *Feiøy* to a place called Træna near the Arctic Circle. I replied what I had said before then Larsen told me and the rest of the crew that the *Feiøy* was as strong as the rocks, and he did not think there was anything wrong with the boat. He continued, "I will ask each one of you on which side you stand, with either Ivar or me, Larsen." So he started with Bjørnøy, Kinn, Olsen, Pletten and Viken. They all sided with me. Larsen was so angry he did not speak to the crew for three or four days.

Then he told the crew that they were taking the *Feiøy* alongside the quay to discharge the cargo. We were to take all the oil drums and spare gear ashore and make the *Feiøy* ready for going on the slipway in

Lerwick. I was not included in the work of discharging the boat but I was asked if I was willing to take the fishing boat *Drott* from Scalloway to Lerwick and then to Peterhead. So I said okay but I wanted two of the boys I had worked along with and also sailed with and that was okay.

So the three of us went to Scalloway and took the boat to Lerwick. The weather was fine when we left Scalloway but when we came around Sumburgh Head we got a strong east-south-east breeze and wet snow. It was just enough for the boat to manage. We arrived in Lerwick and reported our arrival, then we were told to leave that boat and go back to Lunna for another boat, to be taken to Buckie. That was done, but we had a bit of trouble before we could go to Lerwick. But at last we were on our way. On arrival at Lerwick we were told that all the other boats had left early that same morning, so we decided to start next morning, which was Sunday.

We left Lerwick at about 8am and it was a fine day, the sea as smooth as a table top. As there were only three of us we made watches of four hours for each man and that worked out fine. We arrived at Buckie after 30 hours steaming time. It was the afternoon when we got alongside the quay where we had to hand over the boat to the Norwegian consul in Buckie. We got our train ticket from Buckie to Aberdeen where we booked into the Forsyth Hotel in Union Street. We were to stop there for a fortnight as we could not get transport back to Shetland.

When we were in Aberdeen a Norwegian passenger ship, the *Galtesund*, came to Aberdeen. She had been captured by some of the Linge boys. The ship had some Norwegian passengers and Germans who had been disarmed and locked up in cabins. We three men tried to get down to the ship, but that was not allowed. We knew some of the men who had captured the ship, as they were in the same unit as us.

At last we got our tickets to Lerwick on the old *St. Magnus* and we were lucky to get a cabin up on deck. The trip from Aberdeen to Lerwick went fine, smooth sea and sunshine. The ship was somewhere between Fair Isle and Sumburgh Head when a German plane appeared and headed for us but the escort ship opened up so the German did not come close enough to do any damage. I was told later that the plane had dropped two bombs but they did not explode but skipped along the top of the water until they went down.

When all this happened the other two men and I were sitting in the cabin playing cards. We heard the alarm sounding, and had a quick look out on deck, but did not see anything, so we went back to the cabin and continued playing cards. Then the alarm sounded again so we went out on deck and saw that the other passengers were standing around with life-belts on. One of the ship's officers saw us three men without lifebelts. He came and talked a lot of bull and to finish he said, "You stupid bastards." So one of the boys said, "Be careful what you call us. You have surely not heard the story about the RAF captain and the Norwegian petty officer. The Norwegian petty officer got a dent in his head and that healed up okay, but the captain lost all his stripes so he had to start again from the bottom. So officer do not be so fast to issue a name to anybody you do not know."

After the *St. Magnus* arrived in Lerwick we went ashore and went to the Seamen's Mission to sleep there. The following morning we went to our office and reported. I was then told that I had to join Larsen on the *Siglaos*. That was okay with me, but I told them that I was not going to lift any heavy packages as my back was still very sore. The *Siglaos* was lying below the refugee camp so I went out there and found the boat, Larsen and crew. They were making the ship ready for a trip.

Larsen said to me that he was going to show me something. He said that we would go over to the slip and have a look at the *Feiøy*. When we got there he pointed to the keel and two planks lying on the ground and asked me my opinion of the damage. My reply was that I had thought it was something which happened after the ship had been ashore on the rocks. I reminded Larsen how I had stopped him from taking the ship to sea, and how angry he had been. I also said that I had more knowledge of fishing boats than he had.

Well, I got a surprise when Larsen held out his right hand and said, "I am very sorry Ivar. I apologise for what happened at Lunna."

Larsen, as I knew him, was a man who did not like to admit when he was wrong, so to give me his apology must have cost him quite a bit.

The *Siglaos* was ready to sail for Lunna where we were to take onboard two tons of explosives, 60 rifles, 40 tommy guns, and a big number of sten guns. We left Lunna on 26th of March for an isle near Frøya, outside Trondheim. The passage over went without any unexpected incident. We saw for the first time a school of whales which kept a parallel course to us but we did not have the speed to keep up with them.

We got into the outer isles early in the morning, and then we ran into thick fog so we had to slow down to just steering speed. We kept a constant lookout on the bow and when the fog eased up a bit we were entering a narrow sound. Right in the middle of it was a big mine. It was my turn as lookout and I shouted to Larsen that there was a big mine ahead. He shouted back, "Shoot the bastard down." But I advised that we steam slowly towards the mine and push it off the ship's side with our boat hooks and that was done. It was a few exciting minutes until the mine was passed and we could breathe easy again.

We arrived at our destination in the afternoon and got our contact. After dark we discharged all the guns and some of the explosives but only about a quarter of the cargo was put ashore. We covered the stuff up then went to another isle and anchored up hoping to find another place to discharge the last of the cargo. The weather got to be a bit awkward for us with rain and a fresh breeze, but we were hoping we could manage to put some of the remaining cargo ashore and cover it up.

About 4pm a small fishing boat came alongside. It was a fisherman and his two sons. They came onboard and asked if we were interested in buying some fish that they had just caught. Of course we would take all of their fish, but we did not have anything to weigh the fish with. It was agreed to pay so much a box full. The fishermen were satisfied with the price they got, then we invited the three men down into the fo'c'sle for a cup of coffee and something to eat. When they came down and saw the guns on the bulkhead, they stopped and turned to the ladder to go up on deck again. But there was no way to go as one of our crew was blocking the way. When they saw the white bread and all the other food on the table they turned, sat down and had a good meal.

Larsen then asked the old fisherman if he could take a load on his fishing boat and put it ashore on an isle we had pointed out for the next dump. He agreed to do so. About 9pm that night, he came alongside and we loaded the boat up with the explosives. The fisherman and his sons put it ashore on the isle we had told them about. They came back and got another load. They got paid in cash and stores that we had and also with two barrels of fuel and luboil, along with three oilskin coats. All the tinned stuff they got was without labels, but some tins had the name of the contents stamped on. We told them that when the tins were empty they should hammer them flat or bury them in the ground.

We left just after the fisherman and his sons went. We steamed at full speed along the coast for a few hours and then were inside the prohibition zone. We kept steaming along until darkness fell then we crossed the zone and headed for Shetland. We arrived there in good spirit with all our fish. The trip had taken us seven days from when we left until we were back at base.

It was not long before we were away on another trip, to a place not very far from the last one. On this trip we had no cargo – only one man to put ashore at a fishing village called Brattvær, north of Kristiansund. The *Siglaos* left Lunna on the 9th of April in the afternoon and we had a bit of a south-east gale when we came clear of land. I had the watch from 8pm in the evening until 2am in the morning. There were two men in the wheelhouse and each had one hour at the wheel. It was a pitch black dark night with rain. While I was at the wheel I looked out through the starboard window and saw two phosphorescent lines coming straight for the ship. I thought it was a torpedo – "This is it." There was no time to sound the alarm either. I watched the stripes coming towards us and when I thought they would hit, nothing happened, so I looked out the portside wheelhouse window and saw two stripes just alongside one another, making a half circle and coming towards us. I then realised that it was two dolphins playing. I was glad that I had not sounded the alarm to get the crew on deck. The rest of the voyage went okay.

When we came into the coast of Brattvær it was foggy with a light drizzle so the visibility was not too good. We made contact with a fleet of small fishing boats. When we came close to them they hooked fast to the railing or anywhere they could get a hold, and threw fish onboard until we had to stop them. We got the distance to Brattvær and then gave each boat crew soap, tobacco, sugar, tins of margarine and butter and some tins of corned beef. They were very glad of that and they told us that there were no Germans or quislings there so it was okay for us to steam in. We got there and our man went ashore. He got into a family and stayed there and when the mail boat came he went with the boat to Kristiansund.

The *Siglaos* left and steamed out on a south-west course until night came and then the course was checked without much alteration. The wind freshened and by morning we had a strong south-west gale blowing. We kept on steaming and when we ran out our distance by about 20 miles I said to the skipper that we had passed Shetland and were on the west or north-west of Shetland as I could see that it was a different motion of the sea. He gave the order to steam the same course as we had done for the last 20 hours. About noon the next day we saw a ship in the horizon and we made for it. It was an Aberdeen trawler called *Conny*. She was fishing on the eastern side of the Fuglefjord bank off the Færoe Islands. When Larsen asked the direction to take us to Shetland the answer was turn around and steam east by south.

After 20 hours we came in on St. Magnus Bay, so we altered course and steamed towards Yell Sound. We arrived back at Lunna on the 14th of April. Now we thought we would have a few days off, but it wasn't to be. We had to take fuel and stores and steam into Lerwick to get the steering compass adjusted. When that was done we left Shetland once more for Norway, leaving on the 18th just after noon.

It was very fine weather with bright sunshine – a smashing day to be out at sea. We had one man to put ashore in the same place that we put the other two men with all the barrels and boxes. But this man had only a transmitter set which was packed in one old suitcase that he got from me. The set had been given to him in a nearly new green, navy officer's suitcase, and he could not travel on a mail boat or train with a suitcase like that. That was just asking to be picked up by the Germans. My suitcase was just the right size and it was made of strong brown fibre.

The man was landed and he got away the same evening. We did not linger on after he went ashore, we just put to sea right away. The daylight lasted well into the night and there was also a moon. The weather was fine and warm, a bit too warm in the fo'c'sle to sleep, so some of the crew took air mattresses and put them on the hatch with a couple of blankets. Others were just sitting on deck chairs or leaning over the bulwark watching the dolphins rubbing their bodies along the ship's stern. This was a fine trip and we thought it would be our last, but no luck for us!

When we came back to Lunna on the 25th we were told that we had one more trip to do and that would be the last. The *Siglaos* had to get fuel, water and a lot of stores. As we had not put any stores ashore on the previous trip, we wanted a lot more to put ashore this time. We had got quite a lot of information about things like that.

We were delayed for three days, but at last we got our passenger and left, this time from Lerwick, on 7th of May. This trip was also to Brattvær north of Krisriansund. When we arrived there we went to another quay and one of the crew and I helped to carry the passenger's gear. He had two suitcases, not very big. We walked along the road until we came to the harbour at Brattvær. We went into a shop there after our man had got a room for the night. When the other crewman and I came into the shop there were only two or three people there, so we asked if they had any fresh fish for sale. The shop keeper said he had two fresh salmon. One was about 15kg and the other one about 9kg. We bought the salmon and he told us that he would send a boat to where we were lying, so that was okay. He also gave us about 10kg of kippers and said as he handed it over to me, "Kippers from Brattvær means good trip west." I then went into his office and told him about the stores we had onboard to give to the people of Brattvær. I asked if he would put it out equally between the people in the fishing village. He agreed to do that.

When the other man and I came back to the *Siglaos* there were two boats alongside and they were loaded down with all the stores we could spare. Some young boys wanted to come over with us but we had to refuse passage. We gave them all our cigarettes, so each man of the *Siglaos'* crew had about 30 cigarettes left out of our private stock of about 700-800. We got away and made for Shetland.

The second night at sea was just like the last trip, not a breath of wind and the sky was as clear as ever. My watch mate and I went off watch at 2am and about 3am I was called up on deck as Larsen said that there was a submarine following us. I stood for a long time and watched, but could not see anything astern of us and neither could Larsen, so we thought it must have been a drift mine. I went back to my bunk and fell asleep, but was called on deck again about 5am. When I came on deck I saw Larsen walking from one quarter to the other with a Bren gun, then I saw the conning tower of the submarine. She was about half a mile astern of us.

We got all our guns ready. We thought the submarine captain was taking a hell of a chance to chase one boat so close to Shetland. We could not have been more than 20 miles from Out Skerries. We could see the land as clear as anything. Then the submarine blew her tanks and speeded up and came alongside us. We then saw that it was a British submarine. The captain wanted to come onboard but we could not get too close. As a matter of fact we were once too close and one of our propeller blades was broken. The captain wanted us to go to Lerwick, but we told him that we were steaming to our base. But we promised to come to Lerwick the following day, so that was fine. We arrived at Lunna on the 11th of May and that was our last trip for the season of 1941-42.

As we had promised the captain on the submarine we went to Lerwick and went onboard the submarine where we had a good drink of navy rum. The captain told us that he had seen us on all our trips in the month of April and now on our last trip. He told us that he had some prisoners onboard that he would have liked us to take over to Shetland. He knew we were armed but he did not know in what way – we might have big enough guns to damage the side of the submarine so he did not take the chance when he was over in Norwegian waters.

The submarine was the *Trident* and she was often in Lerwick. The captain said that he did not want to swap jobs with us. He said the Germans could see us when we were steaming along the coast, but they could not see him steaming beneath the waves.

We went ashore and after a while we went back to Lunna. The following day we went along on a special job. We steamed along the west coast of Yell to pick up driftwood for, as we were told, the army. But we did not find much good wood so we returned to Lunna. We stopped at Lunna for a few days and put ashore the rest of the high explosives, then we got orders to go to Scalloway as that was to be our new base. We arrived there at 4pm of the 16th May, 1942.

CHAPTER FIVE
Shetland Bus to Scalloway

OUR NEW base at Scalloway was at the West Shore where there was a large two-storey building which had been a net loft in peace time. We had a kitchen, messroom, daily room, reading room, exercise room, bath and toilets on the first floor. On the second floor were two big rooms used as sleeping quarters for about 20 men. We also had two Nissen huts with each made into two rooms. In one of the huts there were four shore staff (slip men) and in the same hut, but another room, were three engineers and one man who worked in the armoury. The hut nearest the road was used by the crews of the fishing boats. Some of the men were also living in private houses. The crew of each ship was kept busy on routine repair work, just to keep the men occupied until all the fishing boats got slip and engineering places fixed up in Scotland, since the Scalloway slip wasn't ready.

The boats were placed from Peterhead to Montrose for full overhaul, and when the date was fixed for each ship, it sailed from Scalloway with its own crew. After the ships had been delivered to each of the repair yards the crew then went on leave for two weeks. Most of the men went to London on a hectic fortnight. Two of the other boys and I went to the unit's Water Lodge on the banks of the Thames in Laleham, a small place outside London. I had been there for a week just before my initial training. It was just a ramshackle hut, but we had good fun there.

We went back to London then were informed that we had to go to the merchant navy gunnery school in Dumbarton to learn to operate different small arms and also heavier guns – a 12 pounder and up to four-inch guns. We arrived at Dumbarton railway station early in the morning, and about 29 of us Linge boys were lined up and had to march from the railway station to the gunnery school, commanded by a Norwegian petty officer. We arrived there just after breakfast, but we did not get any breakfast. We only got time to go to our quarters and drop our kit-bags and cases, then get into the parade ground and line up, as there was a British admiral or commander who was expecting to come and inspect the gunnery and the men.

We were lined up on the parade ground for nearly three solid hours and the 20 of us who had arrived in the morning had not had anything to eat since we left London the previous night. We were hungry and we complained to the petty officer who was in charge of us. At long last we were dismissed and we went to the mess for a meal. We got allocated two tables. We had to get two of the boys to serve as peggies to fetch the food and set the table and after the meal to wash the dishes and store them in their locker. The peggies were changed every week.

We got instructions in small machine guns such as Hotchkiss, Coltmarling and Bren gun and then the gunnery instructor told us about the Lewis gun. There were two types of them, both air-cooled, one with a cover over the barrel and one without. One of the men told the gunnery petty officer that he could forget to teach us about the Bren gun, or the Lewis gun as we could strip the guns down and put them together blindfolded. The gunnery officer said, "Okay, let me see if you boys are so good with the guns. Just start and I will look and see."

The whole of us had to strip and put the guns back together, and after all had completed the task the gunnery officer told us that we did not need to sit and look at the gun. But we were to learn about bigger guns – a six pounder, 12 pounder and at last four-inch guns.

At the time we were at Helenslea House in Dumbarton there were no anti-aircraft guns there, only the three types of big guns. After about eight or 10 weeks we went to Ardrossan where we had a chance to use small machine guns on the gunfield and practise firing at a model aircraft which was moved from one end of the gunfield to the other by wire control. We were not to fire direct at the model but a few inches ahead of it. After that we went into a building called the 'Dome'. In there we saw a film about different types of German aircraft and each man had a go with a Hotchkiss machine gun to shoot at the plane. A coloured yellow spot appeared on the white top and side of the dome when the aircraft came in for attack. The man with the gun did not see if he hit the aircraft but he had to keep his gun right in just at the nose of the plane. When my turn came it was an ME 110 bomber fighter and I kept my eye on him until he disappeared. The next to come on the screen was a German Stuka 87. She started a dive-bomb attack and I kept my sight on the dive and also when she finished diving and straightened out. Then the British instructor stopped me and told me that I had kept the yellow spot right on the nose of both of the planes and if that had been real, both would have been shot down. I was the only one who could follow the Stuka's dive-bombing, but about half of the boys did not do too bad.

We then went to use the Colt MK 50 but after about one and a half bolts of ammo the gun jammed. Next was a new anti-aircraft gun, the Oerlikon 20mm. It required two men to put the tension on the recoil spring on that gun – it had a tension of IBS 500 – then the gun was ready to be fired. A man from the merchant fleet and I were picked to do the job. The merchant fleet man got the first chance to fire the gun, each man being allowed 10 rounds. We had to fire at a parachute which was hanging up on a wire. After going so many feet up the parachute was released and dropped a little, then drifted with the wind and you had to try to shoot it down. The merchant man fired all his 10 rounds without a hit. Then it was my turn and I could see the square parcel going up along the wire. I followed it in the sight and then it was released and dropped a bit. The parachute folded out and I kept my sight on the target and fired three rounds, when the instructor put the safety catch on and told me to get out and let the next man in. Out of

40 men I was the only one who could show 100 per cent marksmanship. I could put on the mark as a gunner in the Norwegian merchant fleet with the letters S.S.H. I got the plaque but I did not use it.

I was at the gunnery school until the end of July when I got orders to go to Aberdeen and then to Peterhead to join one of the fishing boats which was there. When I got to Peterhead I was to book into the Royal Hotel as there were five other Norwegians there – two engineers who had been working on the boats and three others. One was the skipper and the other two were coming as crew. I was going as engineer. We had to stay for nearly a whole week until the boat was ready but at last the skipper called together the crew and we took the boat out on a trial. We also got the steering compass adjusted.

The boat *Harald* left Peterhead on a Sunday morning about 9am with orders to go to Burghead. The weather was very fine, a light northeast breeze and everything went fine until we were abreast of Banff, when the engine slowed down. When I came down to the engine room I saw that I could not do anything to keep the engine running as it was a very vital part which had been broken. The only thing was to hoist the sail and sail towards Buckie. We arrived there and the duty boat came out, put a tow rope to us and brought us into Buckie.

I dismantled the broken part to take ashore to the engineering shop to get welded, but as it was Sunday the engineering shop was closed so we had to stay in Buckie for two whole days. When we got the part fixed it was welded on the wrong side so it had to be planed down for fitting in the right position. After that was done it was put on and the engine tried, but the thing broke again. It was taken ashore and welded again. They also made another one so that we would have a spare if the part did break again. We started the engine and left Buckie for Burghead. We were steaming at half speed and we just made Burghead when the bolts holding the part broke. Now I had once more to get engineers on board. I could not get any engineers from Buckie but our 'office' got some men from the aerodrome at Elgin. They did not know anything about fishing boats so we were as bad as before. However I got the broken bolts unscrewed and got some new bolts the same size as the broken ones.

The *Harald* took on a lot of high explosives and a lot of wood – a full cargo. Another ship was there, the *Erkna*, a big iron ship, 85ft long, which was also to take a cargo to Shetland. The two ships were to leave Burghead together, and if the *Harald* got into trouble again, the *Erkna* would put a towing rope onto her. All went well until the two ships had passed the Pentland Skerry and then the bolts broke. Once more I got the broken bolts unscrewed, put new ones in and started up the engine. It ran for about two or three hours then the bolts broke again. I unscrewed the old bolts, put new ones in and the engine ran for another four hours. I do not remember how many bolts I changed – until I did not have any left. Now the *Erkna* just had to tow us to Scalloway.

It was Sunday morning when we arrived at Scalloway, a lovely morning. I went around the winch looking for a couple of bolts so I could get the engine started so we could steam into the harbour and get alongside the Blacksness Pier. The *Erkna* slowed down and started to heave in the towing rope, then I started the engine on the *Harald* and the skipper told the crew to let go the rope. We steamed at slow speed and got along the quay and made fast. Then the engine stopped again. The *Erkna* came alongside and the skipper came onboard as mad as the devil. He thought we had got him to tow us from Pentland Skerry to Scalloway on purpose. I took him down to the engine room and showed him all the broken bolts and the last two bolts that I had taken from the winch. The crew of the two boats then went ashore. The skippers and three other boys were put into one of the nissen huts. Most of the rest of the boats' crews were put in Norway House.

On Monday the cargoes of the two boats were discharged and the engineers began working on the engine of the *Harald*, put new bolts into the parts which had given so much trouble, started the engine and ran her alongside the quay. The engine ran for about 15 minutes then the bolts broke again. They did the same as I had done in Buckie, opened the fuel filter and found that clean, put new bolts in and started again, with the same result. They stripped the fuel pipe from the fuel pump and also the fuel injector and the fuel safety valve, then they found what the trouble was. The safety valve was screwed up so hard that when the fuel injector got a slight choke the valve did not open up to let the extra pressure off. That was the cause of the broken bolts, but it took the engineers two whole days to find out.

After a while the crews got back to base and the skippers started to gather their men. I had been sailing with Larsen the past season and he expected me to sail with him the next. But the trouble was there were not enough engineers. Larsen had three men who were engineers but August Nærøy did not have one. Nærøy asked me if I would go as engineer on the *Heland* with him, so I said yes. That was okay with Nærøy and he asked me what I thought Larsen would say. My reply to that was that Larsen still had two engineers and I thought that was enough for him.

When I told Larsen that I was going with Nærøy he got most hellish angry and said to me, "Ivar, I thought that you were my man." I told him that he still had two engineers whereas Nærøy had none. Larsen did not get over that. He hardly spoke to me when he was sober, but when he had a drink he would talk about the trips we had done, then he saw the reason why I went with Nærøy.

So I went onboard the *Heland* as engineer. Her engine was a twin-cylinder hot bulb engine. It was the only 85 hp engine from that engineering firm and she was something out of the usual. The *Heland* was made ready for a long trip to an isle south of Bodø called Træna. We started on the trip on the 9th of September, 1942 but had to return after two days out. The trouble was that the reverse bearing ran hot. When we came back to base the engineers did a job on the whole reverse unit and we did a lot of trial runs. Everything seemed okay, so we were ready to take another trip to the same place.

The *Heland* left Scalloway on the 2nd of November. The trip went

Heland. © North Sea Traffic Museum, Telavåg.

fine until we were nearly abreast of our destination when we got a south-east gale. When the *Heland* was running afore the sea, the reverse bearing column vibrated a lot and I could not do anything to stop it. On the morning we were going in towards Træna, the reverse bearing housing cracked with the result that the propeller blades swung from ahead to full astern and the only thing to do now was to strip the whole column off.

I had to try to bring the propeller blades to a head pitch. It was a difficult job sitting across the propeller shaft trying to unscrew part of the reverse gear with the ship rolling and the shaft turning now and again. I got trapped by the shaft and, being in the engine room alone, I could not reach a short pinch bar to turn the shaft to release my legs. Eventually I did get just a little less pressure on my leg and got clear. I finished stripping the reverse gear then went up on deck and forward to the fo'c'sle where the crew was sitting drinking coffee. I told them that I was lucky to manage to get out from under the after cabin as I had been under the cabin deck for about two hours and none of the crew had bothered to come and see how I was getting on. I had my coffee and a cigarette then I told the skipper and the crew what I planned to do. If that was a success we would steam back to Shetland because we could not manoeuvre among the isles we were bound for. But if there was no success we would have to try to make for Træne, discharge the cargo and then blow the *Heland* to bits.

That was agreed so I went down and worked for over two and a half hours. It worked but there was not much of a forward pitch on the propeller wings so the pitch had to be reduced. But what could I use? I did not have any small thin steel wedges but I knew there were some very dry birch lumps in the skipper's cabin. I went there and took two of the lumps and split them to make wedges. I then removed some of the washers that I had used and put two wooden wedges in, one from the top, the other from the bottom, then tightened up the reverse shaft. Eventually we had the right propeller pitch. We steamed for four hours then I had to adjust the pitch again.

We steamed back to Shetland, a distance of 580 miles, and when we came into Scalloway we went straight to our mooring. The men onshore thought it was a strange way to behave, so some of them came out and asked what the trouble was. We told them that the skipper and I were very fed up with the engine. There was a boat lying in Scalloway with a nearly new 50 hp Wichmann engine and we wanted to get that engine and put it into the *Heland*. But it so happened that the owner and skipper of the *Heland* was also the shipwright on the base and he did not want to change the engine – it had been constructed by the shipwright's uncle.

The *Heland* was out of commission while the engineers made a complete new reverse system and eventually she was ready for a trip again. She was lying at Blacksness quay taking fuel when we got a message from the *Askel*. The crew had left the ship as she was sinking, 100-120 miles north-east of Shetland. The *Heland* was made ready to go to assist and pick up the crew.

We left Scalloway about 2pm. The skipper got orders to go north and then go to Baltasound for further orders. When the *Heland* got around the north point of Unst, she got a south-south-west breeze and the tide against her so the speed was not great. We met a British M.L. and they told us to carry on in north-north-east course for about 100 miles, then start to zig-zag about 10 miles on each side of the north-north-east course line. We ran the distance and did the zig-zag but we could not see anything, not even a piece of wood. When it got too dark for searching we stopped the engine and just drifted, but we kept a good watch the whole night.

At about 6am we saw a ship about half a mile away on our port side. I started the engine, but before we could do anything the ship steamed away and was lost to us. We did not know what nationality the ship was but we were nearly sure it was a British destroyer. We started our search again but saw nothing. We stopped to sink a drifting mine, when we saw a destroyer about five miles off. It came steaming towards us, so we thought it was best to leave the mine to drift along. The destroyer started to signal to us to come alongside, so we answered that the sea was too rough. We then got the order to come alongside or they would sink us with gunfire. We opened up our hatches to get our fenders up. We were so close to the destroyer that its guns could not bear on us. We heard a hell of a shout from the destroyer as the men on her thought we had torpedo tubes and were going to sink her. When they saw that it was just a big fender order was restored again among the crew.

Just before we got alongside I went down to the engine room and filled the two lubricators for the engine. Then the skipper came and told me to come up on deck. I was no sooner on deck before I had the barrel of a tommy gun pressed in my back. The skipper said, "It is no use talking to the officers. The bastards are so pig-headed, they think they own the whole bloody ocean."

After going across to the destroyer we were then taken below and our sparky, my second engineer and myself were put into one cabin. They made a search on us and found British cigarettes and a lot of British money (we had been given our leave pay), but they did not take either the cigarettes or the money. The fellow who was in charge of us prisoners was one of the idiots that I had seen wearing a lieutenants' uniform. He was so excited that he came into the cabin where we were held prisoner holding a big revolver, a 38. calibre Webley on a lanyard. He took that off and threw the revolver on top of a desk behind the door then was out and away. The sparky noticed the gun. I was speaking to the sailor who was standing guard on us. The poor bastard stood there and looked right down the barrel of the pistol. I asked him if he had much experience with this sort of gun and he told me this was the first time he had this sort of gun in his hand. I said, "Then do not look down the barrel of a gun like this one or you might get another eye which you won't be able to see with."

Then the two and a half ringer, or two and sixpence as they were called, came over to our cabin. The sparky asked him if he thought that we were Germans. He answered that he was quite sure about that. When I heard that I picked up the pistol and handed it to him with the pistol grip towards him. I said, "This pistol holds five rounds, and the sailor outside our cabin would have been easy to take care of." He took the pistol and disappeared.

About half an hour later we were told to come and get some food. But we did not get into the mess deck before we were called on to the deck to see where they were going to sink the *Heland*. We said that they should take the guns off the boat since they were new. The order came that they were not sinking the *Heland* just yet. We were put back to our prison cabins and the two and sixpence came into our cabin and asked what we were doing out on the ocean. Our answer was that we were doing the same as the destroyer. So he asked what they were doing. We looked at him and said, "Do you not know what you are doing out on the ocean? The best you can do when the ship gets back to base is to go ashore and never to put your big flat feet on a ship's deck again." He got angry. The two sailors who were standing guard over us five men could not laugh, but it was very hard for them to keep a straight face.

Then we were once more ordered up on deck as the *Heland* was going to be sunk. The guns were turned towards the boat where she lay, slowly moving astern against the sea and the fresh wind. We were standing there on deck and we noticed that no order came to open fire. Things started to move faster. Two crewmen of the destroyer came dressed in rubber boots and life jackets. They made one of the whale boats ready and started to lower it level with the deck of the destroyer. Then we were ordered to go on board.

The men were to take us back to the *Heland* and see if she could make Shetland. She was okay when at last we got onboard. True to the navy, you had to board a ship in the same direction of the ship's tow. That could have been okay if the *Heland* had not been going slow astern and against wind and sea. The whale boat came up astern of the *Heland* and got under a quarter of the ship and then went past her. There was not a chance to get onboard that way. The whale boat's crew made three attempts to get alongside the same way. Our skipper then said, "Come up towards the bow and then come alongside portside and put a line onboard." So that was done and we jumped onboard when the whale boat was on top of a wave. The skipper and I were the first to get onboard. I went down in the engine room and checked if there was any water in the bilges and found there was none. So the *Heland* had not got any damage. The destroyer signal man who had come over with us sent the signal that the ship was okay.

Our skipper explained that the commander of the destroyer had told him that he had got an order from our headquarters through Scapa Flow. He had to see if the ship was damaged too much to get back to Shetland. If she was they had to take all the guns, the radio and Admiralty set. When the boat was stripped and the guns and the crew's gear taken away, then he could sink her. But if she could steam back to Shetland then he would have to let her go. The last message from the commander to our crew was, "If I ever happen to meet you and your ship I will sink you without warning." After he said that he saluted our skipper. As he was not a navy man he just calmly replied, "That is okay with me and my crew." The commander did not like such an answer but he did not say anything. The whale boat went back to the destroyer, was picked up and the destroyer steamed away and left us to ourselves.

There was some damage done to the top rail and also the boat deck, and the after mast was standing at an angle of 100 degrees to port. On the fore end of the boat deck a davit for heaving up the lifeboat was missing so that put the steering compass out. We were steaming a course south-west, as it would have been for Shetland, but we were actually steering straight down the middle of the North Sea, about 90 miles east of Shetland. We steamed the course until 10pm. That was only five hours after we got back to the *Heland*. We were prisoners for over four hours on the destroyer.

The skipper tried to take a reading but he could not get a clear horizon, so we steamed the same course at half speed. About 3am the skipper and the sparky each got a good reading of the stars. They found out where we were and the course was altered about south-west and we steamed that course the whole day, as the wind increased in force. About 8pm we got a clear sky and the skipper got another good reading of the stars, and the course was again altered a little. The wind fell away and we got a fine smooth night, but very dark. Just after midnight we saw a darker shadow and found out it was land. We had come in on the south side of a big bay so we started to follow the low shadow then came to a high headland and a point. We started to steam back the way, as we had come right to the point when we first got land. We decided to steam half the distance and then stop and dodge until morning.

After we stopped and were lying dodging at very slow speed we noticed a light on top of the black headland. We had never seen any light on any of the hills in Shetland so it was a bit strange, but we could not pinpoint where it was. We were sure we would find out when daylight came, and we did. When the daylight came the wind freshened to a south-east gale. I was on watch in the engine room. I thought I would have a cup of coffee so I went up to the galley and made some.

When I was waiting for the kettle to boil I was standing looking out the galley door, then I thought I knew where we were lying. I went up to the wheelhouse, out to the chartroom and had a good look at the chart of the north end of Shetland. To my surprise I should have known the area where we were lying.

I did not say a word of what I had discovered but went and called the skipper and told him to come on deck to see if he could recognise the land around us. The first he noticed was something like an M.T.B. coming steaming towards us. It was the same thing that I had seen first. I said the M.T.B. would be there for ever. We had passed that skerry a lot of times going on trips and coming back. We then went up to the wheelhouse and chartroom and I pointed out the isle of Yell. Now we knew where we were. We started to steam for Lerwick. About the same time as we set off the old *Earl of Zetland* came out from Mid Yell, so we had a race with the steamer and arrived in Lerwick about the same time.

When we arrived in Lerwick we had to report the sad news that we had not found the *Askel* and our search had to be abandoned after we were taken prisoner on the destroyer.

When the search party from the destroyer was aboard the *Heland* they ripped the contact terminal off the batteries for our receiver and transmitter and short-circuited the batteries, so there was not a spark of power in them. I connected them up and put the battery under the charge but it did not seem to be any good. The battery was on charge for 36 hours before they started to take charge. The water in the battery was getting low so I ordered four gallons of distilled water. When the cases came onboard I thought it strange that they were sealed. I broke the cases open and I got a surprise for in each case were two one-gallon jars of navy rum. Well, this was something very good, so I told the crew to find all the empty bottles and fill them up with rum. I had a quarter-gallon flask for distilled water that I used when I was topping up the batteries, so I filled the flask half-full and I took the rum and spilled some on top of the batteries, so you could smell the rum. We did not have enough bottles but we used a big kettle, which could hold a gallon, and two pans. So now the four-gallon jars were empty and not too soon either, for the quartermaster came back and asked if I had got distilled water. I said yes, but the distilled water that we used to get was clear, whereas the stuff now was dark brown and smelled like rum. I said I did not know how that would work on the batteries.

The quartermaster said it was a mistake, the two cases were navy rum. But he had four gallons of distilled water. If I wanted them I could have them, but he wanted back what was left of the rum. So I brought the flask with maybe a quarter pint in it. He asked if that was all that was left. I replied, "Yes, and here are the empty gallon jars." He did not want them. He said I could smash them up when we were out in deep water. That was just what I wanted. After the coast was clear we poured the rum from the big kettle and the two pans back into the gallon jars.

While we were at Lerwick we got the after mast put back in the right position and after two and a half days we went back to Scalloway. Then it was decided to send some of the crew on a short holiday as one of the boats was to go to Buckie and the boys from the base were going as crew. The ship set off and made for Buckie, where after a hard punching trip it was handed over to the Norwegian consul there. The boys went by bus to Burghead where the unit had another base. We stayed there two nights and then were put into Elgin to get the train to London. The journey from Elgin to King's Cross station in London was a bit hectic but we arrived in one piece.

We were in London for a week and then returned to Burghead where another crew with their ship had arrived. They left there the same day we returned and took their ship back to Scalloway.

We were delayed with a north-west gale so we could not get out of the harbour. But at last the weather moderated and started to blow from the south-south-west, so we got out with high tide.

The *Feie* got a good run from Burghead to abreast of Orkney when the wind went around to the west-north-west and increased to gale force so we altered course to pass east of Fair Isle. We got to the south end of Fair Isle about 6am. The *Feie* did not make much speed as the sea was very bad. When the biggest breakers came we had to slow down until we were on top of the wave. From the south end of Fair Isle until we were about eight miles north-north-east of the isle, we had taken nine hours for a distance of 11 or 12 miles. The sea was so bad that we could not get the galley fire going so we could not make any warm food. To boil the coffee kettle we used a blow lamp, one man holding the kettle steady while the other used the blow lamp on the bottom of the kettle. Eventually we got the coffee made and that was all the hot stuff we had.

The gale was strong west-north-west and the tide was running against the wind and the sea, and as we did not have that much speed we were forced to the west and a little to the north. Just before it was too dark to see land, we found we were to the west of Fitful Head so now we had to steer east by north to get near land.

The wind fell away, but it was no use to us then because it started to snow very heavily. At times we could not see the mast which was only about 35 feet from the wheelhouse. It was then decided to heave to for the night and we swung around to the west with the engine running dead slow – just steering speed. It was now New Year's Eve and we did not have a dram, or any chance to get a cooked meal. So it had just to be coffee.

It was snowing the whole night, just enough to stop us from getting into Scalloway. About 8am we started to steam towards land, and it was about 10.30am before we saw anything. We made the right entrance and came into Scalloway about noon on the 1st of January, 1943. We moored along the West Shore jetty and went up to Norway House to get some food. We did not see any of the boys of the base. The only ones who were on duty were the cooks. We came into the mess room and asked for something to eat and we got a very good dinner. After having a good meal we went back onboard the *Feie* and brought our stuff ashore to our billets. Then we had a good bath and slept until teatime. Once we had our tea some of us went to the sergeants' mess for our New Year's drink. The sergeants' mess was the only place we could get spirits. We could also buy whisky or rum from some of the staff in the NAAFI canteen, but there were too many who knew about that so the quantity was limited.

Chapter Six

The Last Sailings with Fishing Boats

AFTER OUR New Year celebration we had to get the *Heland* ready for sea again. So we filled up our fuel and water tanks and added a lot of tinned stuff. We were to load a cargo of heavy herring barrels. When we were loading them onto the boat one of the barrels burst open and a lot of coarse salt poured out. A fisherman came over to the boat and wanted to buy that barrel. We told him the salt would be put into another barrel and I am sure that he would have got a 'hell of a surprise if he got the barrel. The salt was just packing for clock mines. The amount of salt was not much more than a quarter of a barrel.

At last the *Heland* was ready and this time it was going to be a long trip, so to save fresh water we got 20 dozen bottles of Pale Indian Ale. That was not something new, but of course we did not say no to a supply like that. So the *Heland* left Scalloway on the 6th of January, 1943 for the west side of the Lofoten Isles in the north of Norway, to a small inlet called Stokkvik, where we were to pick up Hartvik Sverdrup, the owner of some islands there.

The *Heland* steamed away at good speed and there was nothing wrong in the engine room. This was the second trip that we had not had any trouble with the engine. When we were about 130 or 140 miles north of Shetland we sighted three masts eastwards of us, and whatever it was it would be too close to our course. When the skipper went to the chartroom to take the binoculars he found that someone had been onboard the night before and pinched them. They were only brought onboard the night before we left. We altered our course so we were steaming in a big circle to avoid getting too close to the ship, but we were near enough to see that it was a big oil tanker. In other words a supply ship for submarines, and the course he was steaming when he passed us was for Iceland. When he disappeared over the horizon we went back on our right course again.

The weather was very fine for the first of January. The sky was really too clear and the sea too smooth, but we did not see anything unusual. After four days steaming the skipper got a reading of the stars and found out where we were. The course was set for Lofotveggen which is also the name for the west-side of the Lofoten Isles. But where in that wild coast was the small inlet of Stokkvik? At our first try we did not find it so we steamed farther north and found that we were too far north. We slowed down for the night and we were dodging until morning, but when daylight came we did not recognise the shoreline, or the hilltops from the night before. We noticed that it was a very strong north going tide so we started to steam back, and it took us nearly the whole day to steam back to where we stopped the night before.

We searched along the coast for the remainder of the day, and that night we kept speed on the *Heland*. When daylight came we started steaming along the coast. There were two men up in the crow's nest and about 3pm we spotted a hut up in the slope of land. We steamed closer and found the entrance to a fine bay. When we sounded our foghorn a man came out of the hut and started to wave his arms. We put our small boat on the water and two men pulled ashore. The man was Hartvik Sverdrup and he had been in the hut for 10 days. He did not have much gear to bring with him, just one sort of big cardboard box. It had been a box for matches. As a matter of fact, it was about half-full of packets of matches, and a lot of Norwegian money in notes. How much we did not get to know.

We left Stokkvik just before darkness and steamed out from the coast so we were clear of the opening between the south point of the Lofoten Isles, and the isles of Røst and Værøe, as in that area there is a very strong tidal current. We were getting along fine. Now it was a bit of a long lazy swell but no wind.

The first day after we left Lofoten we were maybe about 90 or 100 miles south when a big German plane came over us. It was probably a scouting plane. When the alarm went one man got down to the skipper's cabin to get Sverdrup on deck. He had to carry him up as he was seasick and was not interested in anything. The plane likely made for base and even if we had not fired one shot, the guns had to be inspected to see if they had got any sea water in them. I had the double Colt Mk 50 aft so when I was asked if I had the cover off my guns I said no, but I had elevated the gun in top position. I was asked why I had not taken the cover off. I said that that plane did not carry guns or bombs, so that was the reason. From then onwards we did not see anything, but we kept about 150 to 180 miles from the Norwegian coast, out of patrol plane routes.

We arrived at Scalloway on the evening of 16th of January and the first thing the skipper did was to report about the oil tanker we saw on our way north. Then he reported the missing binoculars, but when the question came up no-one had been onboard the *Heland* the last night before she sailed, so the case was closed. The boat got new binoculars but the skipper kept the case of the old ones.

The *Heland* got a rest now and the crew did the spring cleaning in the fo'c'sle just to pass the time away. Below Norway House, at the corner of the road, was the boiler room. The fuel was wood and one of the crew had a job to cut this wood into suitable lengths for the fire. He was cutting away at the wood when he said he found the *Heland's* lost binoculars. He did not tell anybody at first but somebody spotted him with the set and asked him where he had got them from. He said that it was the ones from the *Heland*. The set was returned to the skipper and since he had a case for the binoculars onboard, the vessel now had two sets.

The *Heland* had been put on the slipway at Scalloway and while she was there we had a daily visit from an American officer. We called him the salvation general. He used to come onboard about 10.30am, about the time we had a coffee break, so we invited him for a cup of coffee. As he talked with the crew down in the fo'c'sle he was aking questions about what we were doing. First of all we showed him a poster which said, "Careless Talk Costs Lives", but he did not take any notice of that. He just kept on asking questions. We told him a lot of rubbish and when he came the next day he got another story, and so it went on for four or five days.

When he went into the office at Dinapore he said to Major Rodgers,"What a lying crew that is on the boat which is standing in the slip. I asked what they were doing. Well, the first story was that they were running supplies to the isle of Foula and to the isles of Rona, St. Kilda and Sule Skerry west of Orkney. They all stuck to that story but they also told a story that they at one time were to put stores on the small rocks in the middle of St. Magnus Bay, but there was nobody to receive the stores so they kept them and put them ashore on Sule Skerry. I have never in my life met such a load of liars. I can only say for that crew and all the rest of the sailing crews that their fighting spirit is okay. But I am sorry to hear rumours that the service is to be stopped because of the heavy losses this season. I feel sorry for the boys, or shall I call them men, as I understand they do not want to join the regular forces. All as one they detest the stiff rules and regulation of the forces. One of the boys said he would not like to be walking and waving his arms like a "bloody windmill".

He was right about the losses. Since moving to Scalloway we had lost three boats and their crews and another boat had been sunk by her crew.

The *Heland* was now ready for another trip and we got stores and some stuff to put ashore at the isles of Skorpa, south-west of Ålesund. We left Scalloway on the 1st of February, 1943. The weather was fine, with just a slight southerly breeze, but it was very cold when we came near the Norwegian coast. We were only about nine hours from Skorpa, when a German Stuka 87 dive-bomber spotted us and came and circled around us for a time. The plane was so close to us that we could see the pilot smiling and pointing towards the coast.

The skipper then stopped and we decided what to do. We decided to dodge until it was dark enough to return to Scalloway. We returned to Scalloway and were welcomed with these words, "August Nærøy and Kaare Iversen must be the most unlucky men." The skipper replied that he and his crew were the most lucky ones, to be still free men, as he heard on the radio in the morning that the area from Stad to Ålesund was a closed area and every boat in the area had to be stopped and searched. If we had been stupid enough to run to our destination, we would surely have been stopped and then we would have to fight, and the result would be in favour of the Germans. We were back in Scalloway and that was the main thing.

Later in the month, when a German patrol plane spotted a ship, they did not attack but followed the boat and plotted the course it was steering. Then they reported to base, and an area of about 50 miles was declared out of bounds and any ship in the area was to stop on signal.

The *Heland* was back in Scalloway on the 5th of February and that was her last trip in the "Shetland Bus".

Now a new operation was required for the fishing boats, to be rigged out for towing midget submarines. The two ships picked for that job were the *Feie* and the *Heland*. They had to go to the west coast of Scotland to a sea loch where the mother ships of the midget submarines were lying. The two boats left Scalloway one afternoon with a south-west breeze, not too strong when we started. The *Heland* was in the lead and the course was set for west of Orkney.

The following morning when it was light enough to see the *Feie*, we noticed that the engine put up a light blue smoke, so we turned back and asked what the trouble was. We got the answer that the ship had sprung a leak, so we got a towing rope and the skipper told the crew of the *Feie* to put up all their sail to help get as much speed as possible.

Towing got underway and after about two and a half hours the towing rope parted just at the bow of the *Feie*, about five to ten fathoms from the ship. The crew on the *Heland* got the 50-fathom towing rope onboard, put a heavy truck tyre at the end and went down close to the *Feie*. We told her crew to make the end of the towing rope fast to the tyre as that would work as a buffer. When that was done the crew of the *Heland* paid out the towing rope and the tow was on again. The engineer on the *Feie* did not even try to use the emergency pump when the engine was still running. He put his attention to getting the lifeboat engine started as it was a failure.

The crew took turns in pumping with the deckpump but that did not stop the *Feie* from sinking slowly. But we managed to take the vessel into the sound between Eday and the Calf of Eday, where the *Heland* anchored and got the *Feie* alongside. We put a hose onboard and started to pump the water out of the *Feie*. We were winning. The water level was sinking rapidly in the hold when the engineer of the *Feie* saw the handlebar of his pushbike sticking up beside a fuel barrel. He gripped hold of the suction hose and pulled it out of the water. After that we could not get the pump to take again, so it was decided to run the *Feie* ashore.

As only one and a half planks were above water, all the gear was put onboard the *Heland* and we raised the anchor and steamed towards the shore right below the lighthouse on Eday. When we thought the *Feie* had enough speed to run ashore we cut the towing rope, backed off and waited until she stopped on the beach and she listed to starboard. The *Heland* then went out and dropped both anchors as it was such a strong tide running through the sound. At ebb tide the skipper of the *Heland* and I went ashore to see what damage she had got. There was an opening on the port side between the keel and the garboard stroke, so big you could put your whole head in. The biggest opening was under the fo'c'sle and it got less when it came to the main mast, so it was a wonder that we had managed to save the ship.

The crew of the *Feie* came onboard the *Heland* for the night, and early the following morning a tug from Scapa Flow came to Eday to take the *Feie* and her crew away. They took all the gear belonging to themselves and the *Feie* and put that onboard the tug. The *Feie* was taken to Buckie for repair. The *Heland* then steamed to Kirkwall to get some stores and also to get permission to go to Inverness and then through the Caledonian Canal, instead of going down the west side of Scotland. The request was granted and the *Heland* left Kirkwall in the late afternoon. We had a fresh west breeze and arrived in Inverness in the late afternoon, but we were too late to go through the Caledonian Canal.

In the evening the crew went ashore to the pub. The sparky and I landed up at a dance. We had a great time there, and when the dance was over we were invited home with two girls that we had talked to and also had a drink with at the pub. We went along with the girls and came to their house where there was a welcome from the girls' mother, whose husband was in the army somewhere in Africa.

The mother made tea and cakes and the five of us had a bit of a conversation going for a while. Then the mother bade us goodnight and went to bed. We did not stay too long after the lady of the house had gone to bed. We stayed maybe for an hour, but nothing happened – perhaps a little kissing and necking, but that had to come to a stop. We told the girls that we had enjoyed the evening with them, and we were sorry that we had to leave as we had to sail early in the morning. We had to be ready about 6am.

We got onboard and turned in for a few hours sleep. The skipper came to call me, but I was already up and the coffee was made. I had a cup and then went to the engine room and started the engine. Now we were ready for the Caledonian Canal. At each of the canal locks we came to the people who worked there asked if we had any spare sugar and tea as they were short of that stuff. We had plenty of those things, so we were dishing out sugar and butter and tea, and we got eggs in exchange. By the time we were on the last lock going up, we had surely about two boxes of eggs, and we also had three boxes from Eday, so now it was eggs and more eggs.

We arrived at the last lock near Fort William but there was no place to go ashore there. There was only one hotel and all they had was sour beer and no spirits. The lieutenant who was a passenger with the *Heland* was told to book a taxi for us, as we were hoping to get to Fort William. But when the lieutenant arrived at his hotel it started to rain a little so he did not book the taxi. Before he left the boat he told us that the engine must be started about 5.45am as we were to leave sharp at 6am. We had a walk ashore but when we could not get good beer or spirits we went back and played cards for a while until we were fed up and went to bed.

I was up at 5am, went to the galley and made coffee. When the coffee was ready the skipper joined me for a cup and about 5.30am I went to the engine room and started the engine. Now the *Heland* was ready to sail again.

We waited and waited but no officers turned up so I stopped the engine. The fellow who was cook for the day made breakfast, and when we had our breakfast about 8am then the Norwegian officer came and shouted down to the fo'c'sle. The skipper shouted back and told him that we were having our breakfast. Then he came down and told us that the ship was now ready to sail as he had let go all the ropes from the stern and the headline. The skipper casually told him to go up on deck and put the ropes back to their respective bollards, or he would have to travel by train to Glasgow and find where the *Heland* was. The skipper said to Eidsheim, "Just you remember you and your side kick are just passengers and have nothing to do onboard this ship as I am the skipper here. So get up and put the rope out." Eidsheim then told me to go and start the engine and I told him that the engine was started before 6am. He knew this as the dock people had told him. I said that we had waited for him for over two hours and a few minutes would not make so much difference. I finished my breakfast and then I went down to the engine room and started the engine and in due course we left the dock.

After we left Fort William, Eidsheim told the skipper that he and the officer were taking over the skipper's cabin. The skipper told him there were two spare bunks in the fo'c'sle, and if they wanted a bunk they could use the two bow bunks, as they were the spare ones. It was up to them.

The *Heland* steamed away at good speed and arrived at the north entrance to the Crinan Canal. The crew had made up their minds to have dinner at the Crinan Hotel. Eidsheim had to pay for the dinner for the whole crew along with a few drinks before dinner time. That was the penalty for not ordering fresh meat for the boat and also for him not ordering a taxi for us at Fort William. Well we had a very good meal and also a good number of drinks before we went back to the boat.

We set off about 8am next day and we got through the canal and came out on the other side, then steamed away and came to Rothesay and moored along the navy tender. When the skipper reported to the commander of that ship he was told that the submarine mother ship had sailed to another place in Scotland, so we had to return and find the ship.

We found the loch where the mother ship was moored, but when we were lying there we did not have anything to do. We saw the midget submarines when they went out on exercise and we saw them coming back to the mother ship. Our crew took trips ashore but there was not much to see. There was a big stream in the valley and we noticed that there was a lot of trout in the stream. We were thinking about fishing there, but we did not have any fishing hooks. When we got back to the *Heland* I was thinking about how I could make a hook. I had some thin spring steel so I tried to make a hook, and it was a success with the first try. The hook was very fine, but there was no barb so it would not hold the fish. I had to make a barb and that was done by putting a lump of solder on the hook, filing it down on both sides, and then making the barb with a sharp point.

The following day three of the crew including me went ashore and up to the stream and we saw a lot of fish. We came to a sort of deep hole and tried the fishing gear. For the first part of the day the fish just swam past the hook and the bait. Then a big fish came on the go and that one took off the bait. So I put new bait on the hook and then I was lucky. I got a fish, a fine one about 10 inches long. One of the other boys had a go and he also got a fish about the same size. We caught six fish that day so we had fried trout for our tea.

The following day the skipper, the sparky and I went on a fishing trip. The skipper was first to try for a fish, and the big one we saw the other day came again. He took the bait but when the skipper tried to land the fish he just got the end of the fishing line with a straight piece of thin wire. The hook was not strong enough for the big fish, so we had to return to the ship. On our way back to our small boat we caught up with an old man who came along the road leading a pony pulling a cart loaded with peat. We stopped the man and started to speak to him but we did not get any answer. So we gave him a cigarette. He took the cigarette and stripped the paper off it and put the tobacco in his mouth, so we gave him a packet. He took the cigarettes but he did not say anything, just a grunt and then he started on his way.

We had seen two small farms, so when we were near the first farm we decided to go over and see if we could buy some vegetables. When we came near we saw people working outside the house, but when we went through the gate in the outer fence all the farm people went inside and locked the door. We went up to the door and knocked, but got no response. We tried again with the same result, so we went away. We had a few glances back to the house, and we could see that the people kept an eye on us but they did not come out until we were a great distance away. We thought that the people there were very queer, so we never went back again.

Back onboard the *Heland* we found that the second engineer had tried to start the engine but could not get it started. Now there was not enough compressed air for starting, just enough for the blow lamp. The engine would have to be started to charge up the tanks for starting air so we prepared to start the engine with man power. We put a rope around the flywheel with three turns and each end of the rope was put up through a hole in the deck just for this purpose. I then lit up the blow lamp and heated two hot bulbs then told the crew on deck to start to pull on the ropes while I helped by pulling down in the engine room. The engine started and she took off.

There was so much fuel pumped in when the second engineer had tried to start it that the fuel had to be burned out before the engine could run at idling speed. I had to open up the blow-off valves so the engine room was full of smoke and whoever looked down could not see anything. The skipper called down to me and asked if I was still with them. I had a good laugh. Then when the engine was running at idling speed I started to charge the air tanks. When I went up on deck and the crew saw me they all burst out laughing. The sparky went down to the cabin and came with a mirror, and when I saw myself I could not help laughing too. My brow was black with soot and oil and the rest of my face was more or less blackened. My right eye was black and I felt that I had got a bit of something in it. But it was not very sore – just some black oil. The second engineer got the order to charge each air tank to 30 kg per square centimetre, then I had a wash.

We were away in Scotland for about a month and at last got our chance to tow a midget submarine. Everything was made ready and the *Heland* moved over to position to pick up the submarine. She came alongside, the towing gear was connected up, and the *Heland* steamed slow ahead. The crew paid out the towing cable and took up the weight of the submarine. Then the skipper got a signal from the submarine commander to give full speed as the submarine was going to dive to 90 to 100 feet. We had a telephone connection with the submarine through the towing cable. We could see that the cable slowly disappeared down through the sea but the speed on the *Heland* did not drop very much. The wind was north-westerly and all was fine.

We were towing away fine when all of a sudden two British minesweepers came straight for us. We did not know what to do, but we hoisted the signal that we were towing and the mine-sweepers altered course and gave us a wide berth. We started the tow about 8am, and we had to tow the sub close to the convoy harbour at Loch Ewe. We had to leave there about 2.30am and we were there at the right time. The submarine disconnected the towing cables and was now on its own and we had to winch in the 120 fathoms of five and a half inch manilla cable. The cable was very stiff after the strain that had been put on it, but at last we had the cable onboard. We made back to the mother ship and got a south-west gale so we set all three sails and the *Heland* was logging nine and a half to ten knots.

The wind increased and we had to put secure locking on the rigging screw on the mizzen mast, as the threads on the screw started to strip. That was likely something that had started when we were alongside the destroyer. We came back to the mother ship about 2pm and we thought that our job was done and we could go back to Scalloway. But no, we would have to stop at the mother ship until the next morning. When we were onboard the mother ship we got our stores. Each man got three cartons of Churchman's cigarettes and just before we were to return to the *Heland* we were well pleased with some rum.

The following morning we got word about our towing and how far into Loch Ewe we had gone – just about a mile outside the boom, but we had not been spotted, and no-one knew that a small submarine had come alongside one of the auxiliary ships which was lying there. The submarine made fast to one of the booms for the whale boat, and when daylight came the commander of the sub made his way onboard the auxiliary navy ship to present himself to the ship's commander. The sub commander told how he had got through the boom about 3am and had been cruising around some of the ships in the harbour, but was not spotted. So he made his way to the navy ship where he could make fast.

The sub commander was asked about how he had managed to come all the distance from the mother ship which was about 80 or 85 miles to the north. He said that a Norwegian boat had towed the submarine the whole distance, and the sub had been submerged for 13 hours of the towing time. The sub commander also said that when the *Heland* slowed down and the sub released the towing cable, *Heland's* engine put up a lot of sparks from the exhaust pipe, so he did not stay long to watch the fishing boat, but made for the boom. When he got through he came up to the surface and, as he had said, cruised around the harbour.

That was the story we heard and it shows you that you could creep up to a convoy harbour and create pure hell with the ships. Watch-keeping was not up to standard and the men who had the watch from 4am to 8am would likely have had some awkward questions to answer.

The *Heland* was then allowed to sail and we set off about 1pm. We were about 5 or 6 miles off Cape Wrath when we spotted a drifting mine and we started to fire at it with the Colt 50. After a few bursts the mine sank so we put on full speed. About 10pm we heard a loud hissing noise and we all went on deck to see that our rocket parachute was hanging about 250ft above the boat. The release was in the wheelhouse and one of the boys had by accident pulled the release line to the rocket. That was the first time it was used and it did work.

The following evening we arrived at Scalloway about 9pm and went to our mooring. We went ashore and got the sad news that more boats had been lost after we went down to Scotland. One was one of the biggest boats, the *Brattholm*. She was captured and the crew were taken prisoners. One man was killed by the Germans and his body was put over the side. The only man who escaped the Germans was Jan Baalsrud who made it to the Swedish border after a lot of suffering. The other boat which was lost was the *Bergholm*. She was bombed west of Kristiansund. They had lost one man, the youngest of the crew, but before he was seriously wounded he shot down one of the two German planes.

The loss of these boats and their crews was very bad news for us. It made a strange sort of feeling and we understood that sailing with the fishing boats was finished. The sailing men who were left asked for a faster boat and more guns and they would carry on. But the big question was where could we find fast and suitable boats for our run. Nobody could answer that.

CHAPTER SEVEN

First News of Faster Boats

The days passed, and the crews on the remaining ships, *Heland, Harald, Siglaos* and *Andholmen* were working on their boats, painting and varnishing and doing other jobs which had to be done before the crews went on leave and on different courses.

At last we were sent away on leave. Sparky Nils, Arnfinn and I went to Aberdeen and booked into the Forsyth Hotel. When we were there we bought a buzzer and a torch battery and connected them to the morse key that Sparky had. Whenever we came into our room one or the other would practice sending signals in Morse. The sound could just be heard out in the corridor of the hotel and in the room on each side of our room. This went on for about 10 days then one evening Aberdeen got a massive bombing raid. They said it was the worst raid of the whole war up to then and a lot of houses had been bombed and burned down.

The sparky and his girlfriend were at the Music Hall at a dance when the alarm sounded clear and the two of them came out. The girl saw the glow of the burning houses and said, "It's burning in my street." She ran away with Sparky in chase, but he lost her among all the people who were out on the street. He came right up to where a house was burning and he heard a woman crying and shouting, "Save my baby. She is in the pram in the house." But the firemen did not make a move. So Sparky went up to one of the firemen and asked why they did not investigate if there was a baby in the pram. The fireman asked, "Would you go in and see?" So Sparky said yes, he was just going to do that. In he went to the burning house and he found the baby in the pram. When he tried to get out the front door he could not get the door open. He put the baby back in the pram and smashed the window, then picked up the baby and got out through the window. Then the fireman put the water hose on him so he had to turn his back to the water jet. It was so strong it nearly pushed him close to the flames. Luckily there were some men and women who got on to the fireman who was manning the hose to turn it on the house and not on the sailor. Sparky handed the baby over to his mother, and then he disappeared.

When he came back to the hotel he was as angry as hell and soaking wet. He had cut one finger and his face was streaked with soot and blood. When Arnfinn and I asked what had happened he only told us that he had followed his girlfriend to her house which was on fire. It was then that he had cut his finger and got soaking wet. He would not tell the right story.

We were in that district the next day and we heard a woman talking about the sailor who saved the baby. If they could find out who he was he should have a reward or a medal for his bravery. When Sparky heard that he got in a hurry to finish his pint and get away, so Arnfinn and I had to do likewise. We had a few drinks and when the pub closed we went back to the hotel.

Sparky and Arnfinn lay down on their beds and I was reading a cowboy story when I heard a knock on the door. I did not pay much attention as there were two girls, about 18 years old, who always used to knock on the door when they passed along, so I thought it was them again. I heard another knock so I went and opened the door. Outside in the corridor stood a man in civilian clothes and he had his right hand in his right jacket pocket. He showed me his card and said, "I'm from the C.I.D.", or something like that. I said, "Come in," and when he was in the room he looked around then said, "Where are your transmitters? We know you have been sending messages to the Germans for the last ten days, and last night proved that, as you did not use your transmitter yesterday."

Sparky Nils then jumped up and said the British must think the Germans stupid to send spies into Britain with a transmitting set that could be heard by Tom, Dick and Harry. He said that to find a transmitter they would have to have at least two or three radio cars. We showed him the buzzer battery and the Morse key and sent a word from an advertisement in the magazine 'Men Only'.

The policeman went out in the corridor and down into the dining room. Then he came back to our room and told us to keep sending. He went out on the street and when he came back to our room he said he could not hear the sound when he was outside and it was very faint in the dining room. Sparky then asked who had reported us but the C.I.D. man would not tell, so he left us to wonder who had.

We found out when we came down for our tea. The three of us were sitting at a big table for eight and it so happened that four Belgian sailors shared the table with us. When we came and sat down the Belgians laid down their knives and forks and left the table. We put two and two together and found out that it was them who had reported us. We would have done the same thing if we had heard anything out of the usual, so there were no hard feelings on our side.

We met the Belgians in a pub later and they were blotto. When they saw us they came over and made an apology for what they had done. We told them we would have done the same thing, so they were to forget it. We could not get clear of the Belgians for a long time that night. They insisted on buying all the drinks, and in the end they had had quite enough and two of them fell asleep. When that happened we bade farewell and left them in the pub.

The following morning we met them at breakfast, but they were not looking too well. When they had finished their meal they came into our room with a bottle of whisky so we could have a drink together before they went to their ship. She was to sail that afternoon, so they would give us a drink to prove that they were our friends. I have not seen any of them since, but I have met the policeman who came to our door. I met him in Aberdeen.

Our leave was nearly finished and we went away on our course to Portsmouth for gunnery training. That was done at a fort outside the naval base, St. Drake. I think the fort was called Breakwater Fort. After about 14 nights there, we were put onboard a half-finished cruiser or something like that. She was moored inside the breakwater and acted as a flack ship. We got our first experience with using twin Oerlikon cannon in turrets and I was again lucky with my firing. I shot down the target the first day and also the second day. I was not the only one to shoot down a target, but I was the only one who did on both days.

We were in Portsmouth for three weeks, and then back to London, where we were called to our office at Earls Court. When we came there each man was asked what branch of the forces we would join. But we were not interested in joining any of the forces, as we were quite happy to stay in our unit. The only thing we could ask for was faster boats and more guns. We were then told that it was nearly impossible to get faster boats, so the boys said, "Give us bigger guns and make them double Oerlikon guns. Give us two double sets for each boat, mounted on the deck forward of the wheelhouse, and also a double Oerlikon on the stern, and then we will have something to give the bloody German planes or even coastal patrol boats." We were not going to join any other group of the forces. If we were to stop sailing from Shetland we would rather join the merchant fleet. But we were not allowed to do so, why I do not know.

Thirteen of the men who had some knowledge about engines were then sent to an engineers' training camp. The others, along with myself were sent to Lowestoft to the engineers' depot, St. Luke, where we were to learn about high speed diesel engines. But at St. Luke there was no high speed diesel. It was an old 100hp Dutch heavy duty diesel made in 1930, and a small Lister diesel 40hp and that was not what we were supposed to learn.

We objected to a lot of things. The whole of us were put up into one room about 18ft by 18ft with two tier bunks. At night, when the blackout was put up, we could not get enough fresh air, so in the morning when you got up your mouth felt like a cotton ball. We complained but it was no use. Then we found a way to get enough air into the room during the night. The last two men who came in had to remove the blackout and open the two windows. Now we were okay but that did not last very long. The second morning our old chief petty officer came to call us at 6am. When he came into the room he got very angry when he saw the blackout had been put aside and that the two windows were wide open. He stood there in the middle of the floor and talked away and laid down the law for us. We all sat up on our bunks and smiled and then we started to laugh. The last thing he said was that he was reporting us to the second in charge at St. Luke's.

The next complaint from us 13 was about the condition of the mess deck where about 1800 men had their meals. The trouble was that there was only enough cutlery for about 300 or 500 men. When you got the stuff which was called lunch, you had to stand and look to see if one man was finished with his knife or another with his spoon, then you went and got hold of whatever it was. You sort of washed it in a bucket with dirty greasy water.

The following day Arne and I were appointed to go through to the second in command and complain. We lined up outside the commander's office along with a lot of petty officers. The door was firmly locked, but there was a peep hole. Arne and I could see the big burly man walking round in his shirt sleeves. Soon Arne and I were the only two left in the queue. We decided to act and without knocking we opened the door and stepped inside the office. The big man had his back to the door when we burst in, and he spun round like a big top. Then he started to lecture us. We told him to listen to what we had to tell him. We told him about the conditions on the mess deck and that we were sent down here to learn about high speed diesel engines and we wanted to know where these engines were.

Arne and I did not give a damn for the commander as we had found out that he was just a glorified fireman from one of the Norwegian whale catchers that had arrived in Britain. He phoned our office in London and the man who answered the phone was army sergeant Løberg. Arne and I could see that the commander was highly confused that it was an army sergeant who answered the phone. He started to tell the man in London that he had got 13 petty officers here at St. Luke, but there was only one man who had a petty officer's uniform and he wanted to know what unit the man belonged to. He was told to give the men all the assistance they wanted, and it would be best for him to remember that in the future, or for as long as the men were there.

Arne and I could hear some of the conversation from London, so when he put the phone down we asked him to come along with us to the mess deck. He did not want to come as he said that he had inspected the mess deck not long ago. Arne and I insisted that he had to come or we would start a strike until everything was put right. Well he came along and I can tell you he did not like what he saw there. The 12 petty officers who were mess men did not like it when Arne and I went around to show him the bucket with dirty greasy water where the men sort of rinsed their items of cutlery. Next were the tea urns. Some of the sailors drew off a pint of tea and when it turned cold they put it back into the urn. It was altogether a very un-hygienic mess deck. The commander promised that it would be fixed the same day and I must admit that he got it up to standard.

After the commander had left, the mess men and the sailors gave us some hard looks. We were sure there would be some trouble between us and the mess men. When we came back to the mess deck we got a surprise since the air smelled pure, the mess deck was scrubbed clean and no bucket of water to be seen. In one corner a table with a white cloth was set for 13 men and a Wren stood waiting to serve us when we came in for our meal. Across the deck all the men had knives, forks and spoons so now it was smiles all round. Some of the men stopped at our table and thanked Arne and me for what we did. They also said they were annoyed that these bloody interfering Norwegians were creating hell in the mess deck, but when they saw the result it was okay.

We were put into private lodgings down in a place called Kirkly, near the river. There we were put onboard a naval yacht on the Oulton Broad. The yacht was 40ft long and was powered by a 500hp Thornycroft petrol engine. When we first came there the chief petty officer told us that he had had the same boat for ten years and had had no trouble, but lately he noticed that he used much more air to start the engine than before. He added that he had a good air compressor so it was okay.

The chief petty officer went up to St. Luke's one day saying that he would be away for a few hours. We said that was okay. He had no sooner disappeared when Johan, our chief engineer, said now we had a chance to strip the air starter and clean it up. It was the same system as was on the Norwegian Wichmann multiple cylinder engine. So we stripped the air starter and it was dirty. It was a wonder that it worked at all.

It took us a bit longer than it should have done owing to the dirt. We had started to reassemble the starter when the petty officer came back. When he saw what we had done, he was very angry. Johan started to ask the petty officer if he could explain how this starter worked, and he replied that he had not had the starter off the engine in all the years he had been petty officer. Johan then explained how the starter worked, then the petty officer asked Johan how he knew so much about air starters. Johan explained that he had served his time in one of Norway's biggest engineering plants, the Wichman motor factory, and that he had made quite a number of air starters. So Johan was asked why, if he had served his time, he had not got his engineer's ticket. He replied that he had his tickets as a steam and diesel engineer and that he had served on passenger ships until the war broke out. The petty officer told Johan that he could get a good job in the British navy as an instructor in engineering, but Johan said, "No thank you!"

We were at Kirkly naval base for about three weeks and finished our course. Before we had to go away we had to see a film about a ship that we were not much interested in. We had to go and pretend that we were interested, and when the film was finished we were marched out on a balcony up on the third floor, overlooking the parade ground. The British commander and the second in command, with members of staff, came out and the commander made a speech. He said that these 13 men who were standing here had been sent to learn about high speed diesel engines, but he was sorry that there were no such engines at St. Luke's. Those men were to go to the USA and learn a little bit more about diesel engines. While at Kirkly, they had taught some of the British chief engineers a few things about fast running petrol engines. He said that he was glad that he had met us and he wished us all the luck in the future.

We were browned off standing there as figures for display so when the big boss had left we went to the paymaster to get our tickets to London. There were three of us who had to go from Lowestoft to Aberdeen and then to Lerwick, that was Harald, Arne and me. We got our vouchers for the train fare from Lowestoft, King's Cross, and 'Lerwick railway station, Scotland'. We told the paymaster that there was no railway station in Lerwick, but he told us that we had got our vouchers for the fare and that was that. We told him that there was a passenger ship that ran from Aberdeen to Lerwick. But it was no use arguing with him.

We arrived at King's Cross railway station and when we went to the railway ticket office to get the voucher exchanged for railway tickets and also for the passenger boat ticket, the clerk at the office asked what stupid bastard had made out a railway voucher from Lowestoft railway station to Lerwick railway station. Did the stupid nut not know that Lerwick was in the Shetland Isles about 200 miles north of Aberdeen? Well, we got our tickets, but afterwards I was sorry not to hold on to that voucher.

We left King's Cross about 7pm and the train was fairly full up. We had bought some whisky to drink on the train and also had about half a dozen bottles of beer. We also had glasses so we started drinking. We could see that some of the passengers were looking at us and they likely made some remarks about us. We did not drink very quickly, but took our own good time. It was about midnight before the first bottle was finished and we were still fairly sober. Some of the passengers had fallen asleep, while others were still awake and kept staring at us, maybe wondering when we would start to sing or do something else. As nothing happened that way, we started on our second bottle. They lost all interest in us and one after the other fell asleep. We finished our second bottle and then we settled down to sleep too.

We awakened long before we came to Aberdeen and had a couple of bottles of beer each. So now all the drink was finished and we were clear of the bottles. We walked around Aberdeen and got our gear down to the North boat which was to sail in the late afternoon. We paid a visit to some of the pubs, but we were very moderate with our drinking. We bought some stuff to bring aboard for the journey north.

We arrived in Scalloway the following forenoon, and got into our quarters. Then we were told to start working on the boats' engines, mostly to start the engines, charge the lighting and radio batteries and so on. After a few weeks Scalloway base was again ready for action, although we did not know what was going to happen. We had got our 20mm Oerlikon gun on the fishing boat and Harald and I were out practising with it a few times. The boys were delighted to find how easy and steady it was to use the gun.

The summer was coming to an end and we had not made the first trip across to Norway yet. We were a bit uneasy about what was going to happen at the Scalloway base, although it was rumoured that we were to get fast American vessels.

In September 1943 – or was it the end of August – I was asked to go as a pilot on a Norwegian torpedo boat from Lerwick to near my home place in Norway. I agreed to go, and the same day as MTB 626 was to go on the trip the commander in Lerwick said, "Ivar, I hope that you do come on this trip now, even after your unit has got the three American sub-chasers." I replied that I had promised to go on the 626 and that was that. I was not going to back out – a promise is a promise.

On the trip, one British and three Norwegian MTBs were towed to the Norwegian coast by two Norwegian whale catchers, the *Malde* and the *Horten*. Each of the whale catchers had two MTBs. The tow was rather slow. When we came to the position to be on our own and let go the towing gear something happened to the British MTB. It got fouled in the towing gear and got wound up so she was out of action and had to be towed back to Lerwick. The other three vessels steamed towards their destination and just before nightfall the leading MTB came alongside 626 and told the commanding officer that we had to make land and watch for the German convoy we were to attack. Tamber, the flotilla leader, did not get a clear answer from 626 as we had one of the Norwegian admirals onboard. Tamber went full ahead and the other two vessels had to follow.

As I was supposed to be the pilot and take the vessels into a place near the outer coast, I was called to the chartroom and asked where I would find a suitable place to hide. I pointed out the place and was told that the officers did not know where we were at the time. I said, "You knew where you were when the whale catchers let go of the towing and you know the course you have been steering and also your speed, so it should not be too much trouble to find out where you are at this time."

The admiral said that during the summer months from 1932 to 1938 he was commander of a submarine of the Norwegian navy. They used to go in through this fairway when they had lights to guide them in through a narrow sound passing a shoal and rocks. I said, "That was in fine weather. But you may try to go in on the same place now and you would not know where you are. But if you insist, just go. I will try to get onboard one of the other MTBs as I have been asked to act as a pilot and I know this area as I served on a pilot boat in the same district."

We did not try for that fairway as it was no good and if you did come through you were right under the eyes of the Germans, as they had a lookout post at a lighthouse there. The lighthouse was later bombed. The three MTBs steamed nearly to the place where I had told them that we would go and put the camouflage nets over the three boats, but that was turned down. Instead we were to remain at sea and wait for the German convoy to come along.

The three MTBs were lying in a sort of triangle. The MTB to the north used his aldis lamp to the one in the middle and he then used his lamp to signal to the one in the southern sector of the triangle. When number three again used his aldis lamp towards number two, that was in the right sector where the German coast lookout post was and the Germans thought there was something fishy about the funny lights flashing. So when the German patrol boat got word from three lookout stations they put the patrol boat out to investigate. The German patrol boat came out and up to MTB 626. Just before that I was called up to the bridge and one of the officers said he saw a green flash from the shore.

I knew where we were but I did not say so, instead I asked if they had seen the patrol ship which was coming up on our portside. The MTB was drifting with the main engine stopped. After I had seen the patrol boat the alarm went on the MTB and when the crews got to their respective gun turrets and tried to turn the guns towards the patrol ship, the barrels pointed up towards St. Peter as there was no pressure in the hydraulic system. When the patrol ship did not get a reply to his signal he put out all his lights and started firing at the nearest MTB, but all his shots went high over the vessel. The admiral and the commander of MTB 626 were giving zig-zag courses to steer, running away as scared rabbits. If they had turned and put only one fish in the patrol boat that would have been right. But no. Three fast MTBs with torpedoes and guns ran away from an old whalecatcher armed with one small cannon and a couple of 20mm anti-aircraft guns. To make it worse for us, that evening the Norwegian quisling radio announced that one German gunboat had chased away three ex-Norwegian MTBs and had damaged us very badly.

Back at Lerwick commander Horve came onboard and he said to me, "Ivar the next trip will be better." I calmly answered that there would not be another trip for me on any MTB. I had thought that the MTB was a highly efficient fighting unit, but after this trip I did not think highly of the MTB. I said that I was very glad the boys in the Scalloway unit had got American sub-chasers. I said that if I had seen action from the three MTBs I might have volunteered for another trip but not after I saw what happened.

The other five men from the Scalloway base, and myself, went back to our work in the village. It was just to put in time until the new ships would arrive in Scotland. That took a long time. We knew the vessels had been put onboard big ships as deck cargo and we feared that those ships were sunk and our new ships along with them. At last we got word that the ships had arrived at the American base at Rothesay and that five men would have to go to the Clyde on a submarine escort ship, an old first war destroyer. The men who were picked for our vessel were skipper Peter Salen, chief engineer J. Haldorsen, 1st coxswain O. Hillersøy, quartermaster A.B.P. Haugland and myself as first engineer.

We were delayed for a couple of days before we sailed from Lerwick. It was blowing a south-west gale and when the destroyer was about 8 or 10 miles south-west of Sumburgh Head the action station alarm went off and what a shambles ensued. The lookout had not seen anything, the instruments could not register anything unusual and the alarm could not be stopped. At last an electrician removed one fuse and that stopped the racket. Then the electrician found that a junction box was full of water and that was the cause of the alarm.

After about six hours steaming the destroyer was told to steam towards North Rona. There was a fleet manoeuvre going on from Pentland Firth towards St. Kilda, so the escort with its two submarines had to keep out of the road. Well, the destroyer arrived at Port Glasgow and the submarines disappeared. The destroyer was put to anchor, and on its port side we saw a very big ship loaded with troops. We also noticed that just over the water line forward it looked like the bow was stoved in. We were not that much interested in that, the only thing we were interested in was to get ashore and get to the American camp and see the sub-chasers. At long last we were put ashore at Port Glasgow, and were taken from there on a herring drifter to a long wooden jetty where a U.S. van was waiting for us. They put us right down to SC 683, our new vessel.

The five of us put our gear onboard and then we were introduced to the deck officers on watch. Haldorsen and I were introduced to the American chief engineer, Mr. Brown and his first engineer, Holland. We hit it off right from the start. The American asked us if we had any experience of high-speed diesel, so we had to admit that we had none. They said, "If you run into trouble just get towed along to a repair yard and everything will be made okay." When we told them that there was not any repair yard where we were to work from, they doubted if we were able to operate the engines and also keep them in good order.

The first day, after all the crew had arrived, we were out on a trial run. In the forenoon the American engineer was in charge of the engine and in the afternoon the Norwegian engineer was in charge. There was not a hitch. Everything went as smooth as if we had been working with these engines our whole life. We had three days at the American base where we were mostly out running the boat and studying the engine. The instruction books were very good with pictures of nearly every part of the engine, so if you followed the number of each item you could not go wrong. The boats had a lot of depth charges and also a double battery of small bombs placed on the foredeck, discharged with electricity. They were used against submarines. All the depth charges and those bombs on the foredeck had to be taken ashore, so we had to take the three sub-chasers over to Ireland, to Londonderry, where there was an American naval base.

CHAPTER EIGHT

Fast Subchasers Take Over

T he sub-chasers left the Clyde early one morning, in moderate southerly wind. We had not steamed very far before the American engineer got seasick, then the starboard engine started to pack up. It was water in the fuel. Both engines had 16 cylinders and six of the starboard engine's cylinders were out of running order. The American chief engineer advised us to leave that engine and just steam away only on the port engine, but Johan Haldorsen said that we were stripping the faulty fuel injectors. Haldorsen and I changed six injectors and now we were steaming with both engines. The other two sub-chasers also had water

Vigra. © Norwegian Sea Traffic Museum.

in the fuel and one engine on each of them stopped. They arrived with one engine running.

As soon as we were moored up the Americans from the base in Londonderry came on board and started to dismantle all the stuff which was to be taken ashore. We were in Londonderry for one and a half days then went back to the American base at the Clyde. Next day the flags were changed, from stars and stripes, to the Norwegian navy flag. The American and Norwegian crews lined up on the quay, and after the changing of the flags, the Americans stepped back a few paces and the Norwegians moved forward. Then the American commander of the base formally handed the boats over to the Norwegian officers and crews. These boats which we were now to sail in, were a present from the U.S. navy to our men. He wished all of us good luck. Some of the American crew would have liked to come along with us, but they were not allowed to do so.

We left the Clyde that same evening. Onboard the sub-chaser 683 we had the American chief and his first engineer. They came up to Shetland as guaranteed engineers and we also had one deck officer with us. The trip north was very good and we came back to Scalloway on the second day after leaving the Clyde. The people of Scalloway had heard rumours that the Norwegians were going to get 'gun boats', so when the fine looking vessels came into Scalloway harbour they caused quite a sensation as men, women and children stood and looked for a while. Each of the sub-chasers had its moorings laid already and went there after calling at the pier.

After we arrived we were very busy. The wheelhouse had to be padded and we had to get a lifeboat. We had to rig two davits for the lifeboat and do a lot of other things before we could go out on a trip.

The first trip for the SC 683, now called *Hessa*, was to Sotra, an isle west of Bergen. The trip started in the afternoon 13th of December, 1943 and we were back in Scalloway in the late afternoon next day. The *Hessa* was supposed to pick up a man but he had left the night before we came, so that was not any good for us. The weather was very good with hardly a ripple on the water.

The other two sub-chasers, the *Hitra* and the *Vigra*, had also been out on their first trip. One of the boats got its contact man, while the other was unlucky.

The *Hessa* was put on the slipway to get some work done for a gun mounting for a pom-pom gun on the afterdeck. When the work was done the crew of the *Hessa* went on leave, the cook and I being the only ones left onboard.

The *Hitra* was going on a trip to the isle of Skorpa, south-west of Ålesund, and I was going as gunner on the starboard Oerlikon. We left Scalloway on the 4th of January and got a very bad trip with a strong south-west gale. When we were near our destination the sea was so bad that we did not know what was shoal water or big breakers. I was at the wheel when I got the order to swing around to the west. It was then 6pm at night on the 5th. We could not use much speed, only about 500 rpm and that was just enough to give the boat a speed of five knots.

The crew of the *Hessa*.

We decided to return to Shetland, and by 2pm the following afternoon we had steamed a distance of 85 miles. A course was laid for the north point of Shetland, the wind west-north-west, a strong gale. At 2pm the course was altered so we were now steaming for the south end of Shetland and we got the sea and wind abeam of us. Now we could use full speed, but it had to be with a man at the controls, so if a bad breaker came we had to slow down until we were on the crest of the wave, then give full speed. About half an hour after we had changed course the lookout on the top bridge shouted down through the voicepipe that the last breaker had smashed up the lifeboat and buckled the armoured plating on the starboard Oerlikon gun. Some of the watch had a look but there was nothing they could do.

From 2pm in the afternoon until 9.30pm at night the *Hitra* had steamed about a distance of 135 miles. We got into Lerwick and when the shore officers came onboard they told us that a British submarine had seen a top bridge and a mast with something that could have been a flag. The rest was just a big solid spray. The commander has asked if there was a surface ship from Shetland at sea. He said, "Tell the mad man to get into harbour, and for God's sake do not let them get out into the North Sea."

The commander had just come far enough up that he could use his periscope and then he saw something, he did not know what, and the submarine was rolling a bit so he went down to 40 feet below the surface. The *Hitra* stopped in Lerwick for the night and left for Scalloway the following morning about 8am. When we came out past the boom defence we met the submarine which had spotted us.

Arriving in Scalloway the lifeboat was brought ashore to be repainted. A new side was put in the boat, and the armour plating on the starboard Oerlikon had to be dismantled before I could get it cleaned. After I had finished with that I went back to the *Hessa* and worked with different jobs.

The next trip for the *Hessa* was to a place south of Bergen which was called Drønen of Huftøy. This time we were also to pick up a man. The trip across was fine but very cold. The *Hessa* spotted a fleet of fishing boats and steamed very slowly towards one of them. We came on the port side of the boat. The man who was standing fishing there did not notice at first, the dark-hulled ship with about six black-clothed men, looking down on his boat. When he realised it was a navy ship he jumped into the wheelhouse and put the engine full ahead. Then he shouted to the rest of his crew to throw fish onboard the navy ship. The crew of the *Hessa* did not say a word to the fisherman. He likely thought it was a German ship. After getting our fish we steamed to pick up our man, but he had not arrived, so we went out to sea again. We went back the following night but the man still had not turned up so the *Hessa* returned to Scalloway. We were told that the man had got another place to be picked up at.

The next trip was to Hovda, in Frøysjøen and that trip started on the 9th of March and lasted until the 11th. We had two men and quite a lot of stores to put ashore for them. It took some time to get that discharged but the weather was in our favour and we returned to Scalloway after our first successful trip.

Our next trip was to a fishing village south of Bodø, which was called Lonan. We were to discharge a lot of stores and high explosives there. We arrived at the right time but we could not get any contact with the men who were to receive the stores. We were lying in a narrow sound when the wind arose and it started snowing heavily, so the skipper took the *Hessa* out to sea and steamed about 60 or 70 miles north-west from Lonan. When we were lying out at sea the engineer had to pump fuel oil from the barrels on deck to the main fuel tanks. In the afternoon it was still snowing but not quite so heavy. We steamed back to Lonan and arrived there about 8pm, but there was no contact that night either.

We stayed there from 8pm in the evening until 5am in the morning, when we put to sea and returned to Scalloway. After we got back we were told that the contact man had made a mistake with the time and the date of the *Hessa's* trip. Most of the people of the isles of Lonan were at a wedding. There was one man who said that he thought he had seen a navy ship lying in the sound but the man did not investigate. The skipper and the crew got a lot of sarcastic remarks about the trip.

The *Hessa* was the only one of the sub-chasers whose crew was mostly from the old fishing boats. I can guarantee that the *Hessa's* crew was the best. During the time that the sub-chasers were based in Scalloway we got only one new man. The other two boats had a steady change of deckhands.

The next trip for the *Hessa* was to Sognesjøen, to land two men. The trip started on 7th of April and lasted for one day, back on the 8th. When we arrived at Sognesjøen it was thick fog so the skipper would not take a chance to steam in among a lot of shoals and small isles. The *Hessa* lay drifting, hoping that the fog would clear away, but not a chance. The only thing to do was to return to base again.

The next trip started on the 11th, to Skorpa, south of Ålesund. It was a very fine trip but very cold. We arrived right on time, got all the stores and gear discharged and then we went to sea again. The trip back went very well, but down in the engine room we had a little trouble. The port engine started to lose fresh cooling water – not a great lot, but we could see that it got less in the tank. We knew that we would have a long job on our hands when we were back in base. We had some rest then the work started. After 16 hours the engine was ready again for another trip. This time we were to go to a place called Dombevågen to pick up three men who were on the run from the Germans. We got the men and returned to Shetland. Usually there was nothing to see on the crossing but on this trip we spotted two German E-boats, but they did not know anything about us. The E-boats were steaming in the inner fairway and they were probably going to one of the small townships along the coast.

Another trip started on the 18th April, again to Dombevågen, and we were back at base the next day. We spent a few days at base and most of the time we were out around the isles outside Scalloway, fishing or practising with small guns and arms.

Next the *Hessa* was called out on a trip to Skorpa. This time we had three men who were to be put ashore, along with a lot of high explosives and 12 clock mines. We arrived near the Norwegian coast about 50 miles off our destination. The sea was as smooth as a table top and the sun was shining from a cloudless sky, so eveything was just fine.

At 3pm the alarm for action station sounded and all hands went to their respective stations. The engine was running at idling speed and all the gun turrets were turned on. The four men who had their action station down in the engine room could only listen to the gun turrets, not knowing what was happening. The alarm lasted about 15 minutes, then it was all clear. The cause of the alarm was eleven British Bristol bombers which had been on a raid on the Norwegian coast. Our boys said, "It won't be long before the German planes will be here." They came exactly one hour after the British planes disappeared. It was three German Messer Schmitt 110 fighter-bombers. They circled around us for about 15 or 20 minutes. As the *Hessa* was lying stopped the Germans could not see the flag clearly, so it must have been the leading pilot who fired his recognition signal. The signal man on the *Hessa* was standing with the big Morse lamp and he sent some quick flashes and that fooled the Germans.

As I said before, the four men in the engine room did not know what happened on deck, so when the hatch over our control room was yanked open a very excited face looked down on us and asked for some cotton waste. He got a great bundle of waste, and then he only took just enough to make small plugs for his ears because he could not hear for the scream of the gun turrets. When he first came we thought that some poor chap had cashed in his chips, but it was nothing like that.

After the German planes had left we turned back to base, but the Germans had realised their mistake and they put out a patrol plane. We could see it scouting far astern for us. It did not pick us up as it had started to rain and turned sort of misty. That was the *Hessa's* last trip of the season.

During the summer months the engines were overhauled and the ship had to go on the slip to be painted and inspected. She had one trip to Dundee with two submarines and after that she went to Scapa Flow for gunnery training. We were there for three weeks then back to Scalloway. During the summer the engine was checked to see if we could find any faults. We made sure that there was nothing wrong. We realised that if the ship was over on the Norwegian coast and had to get away at top speed the engine must be in top running order. There were two main engines but you could not force the remaining engine at top speed. That engine would have to be run at a reasonable speed to bring the ship back to base.

In the summer of 1944, the *Hessa* had just had both main engines overhauled and was lying alongside the quay, when we got orders to go out to the isle of Foula. We had to pick up a British airman, the only survivor of a Catalina flying boat. As it was Sunday about half of the crew were in Lerwick at the picture house and so was our chief engineer. We got a crew made up and set off from Scalloway. As the *Hessa* steamed out of Scalloway harbour the bus from Lerwick arrived and our chief engineer saw his ship steam out to sea. He was not very happy at all and began walking from Norway House down to the quay and back. The last time he was down at the quay was about 4am, then he went to bed, quite sure that I had driven the engines too hard and blown them up.

When we left Scalloway I told the skipper that I had to run the engine at a reduced speed until the temperature became steady, then he would get the speed he wanted. From Scalloway to Foula we steamed for one hour and 25 minutes. We arrived at Foula and half the crew went ashore to help bring the wounded airman on a stretcher from the south-west side of the island up the hillside. It took the whole night for the party to arrive with the airman. His condition was not very good, so now the skipper told me that he wanted all the speed he could get right from the start. Well, if the trip from Scalloway to Foula was quick, this trip was even quicker – Foula to Scalloway in one hour and five minutes. The airman was rushed to hospital and he survived, thanks to the speed that he was brought to the doctors.

The chief engineer came onboard before breakfast and the first thing he did was go down into the control room and check the temperatures, pressures and the fresh cooling water supply tank to see if there was any leakage. He did not want to find any fault, but he was not pleased about the way the main engines had been driven from Foula to Scalloway and he said so to me. To hell with the engine, I said. We saved a man's life. I said that if the engines could not stand that pressure – after all the temperature was steady – the engine was not up to what was said. The chief cooled down and he saw the reason for the trip.

The summer went on as usual at the Scalloway base. The sub-chasers had not much work to do – only out for gun training against flying targets and sometimes out to the south-west side of Scalloway to lay smoke screens just for practice.

The time was soon coming to start a new season. *Hessa's* first trip was to Hovda on the 19th August. We landed three men with some stores and transmitters. There was nothing unusual on this trip – fine calm weather. The next trip was to Erkna, near Ålesund. We did not get contact with the man ashore so we had to return to base. This time we saw some fishing boats and stopped one of them. These were small whalecatchers and we got some whale meat and the boat's crew got cigarettes, coffee, corned beef, butter, margarine etc. After that we went back to base.

The next trip for *Hessa* was again to Erkna. We had to put some stores ashore there for the resistance group in Ålesund. All went fine but on our trip back to Scalloway we steamed into a submarine net which was drifting halfway between Shetland and Norway. We were steaming along at a speed of 15 knots. Just as daylight came, the lookout up on the top bridge spotted something like a conning tower of a submarine about two miles away, on our starboard bow. But before the alarm was sounded we heard a hell of a loud crash and one of the main engines stopped. We did not know then what had happened to the port engine so we just had to steam with the starboard engine.

We arrived at Scalloway and when we used a small rowing boat we could see some wire and some floats on the starboard propeller. So the *Hessa* had to go on the slip to clear the propeller. When she was high and dry on the slip we saw that there was some more wire and floats on the port engine propeller. Both propellers were cleared and the length of wire on each was about 12 fathoms. On the port propeller eight floats were crushed flat and on the starboard propeller there were seven crushed flat. The wire was one and a half inches thick. It had not done any damage to the propeller or the shaft.

After coming off the slip the *Hessa* was refuelled and made ready for another trip, which started on 28th August and finished on 2nd September. This was a long trip to Lanan, in Nordland, where the *Hessa* had to evacuate all the people of the isle, a total of 28. The oldest was 65 and the youngest was only about five months old. We arrived at Lanan about 10pm and the first people came onboard about 11pm. They had a lot of luggage to be brought onboard and stored away, so it took some time, but about 2am in the morning the *Hessa* left the isle and steamed out clear of the coast.

A good north-east gale was blowing and the sea was not very rough, but right for us as we were not easy spotted in the broken sea. The passengers were told to remain below deck if the alarm went, so they half-heartedly promised that. But when the alarm sounded about 11am nearly all the men and three young girls were seen on deck. They were promptly put below deck and the cook ordered to see that they did not come up again as long as the ship was at action stations. At last the all clear was given and those who had been on deck complained very loudly because they wanted to see the crew of the *Hessa* shooting down a

German aircraft. It was a big six-engine plane, used as a scouting plane up in the north of Norway, which had caused the alarm.

When the *Hessa* arrived at Scalloway she berthed at Port Arthur, where our passengers were put ashore, then transported to the refugee camp in Lerwick. Some of the *Hessa's* crew went with them to the camp to speak to the people we had brought back, but they were chased away by the guards. The boys told the guards that these people had been on our ship for three days, and that they knew the people and their names. But it was no use.

The *Hessa's* next trip was to Nordfjord on 7th September, back next day. On this trip she carried two small submarines about nine feet long and powered by 24-volt batteries. These small submarines carried limpet mines to be placed on the most vital parts of the ships, under the water line. The small submarines were called 'sleeping beauties'.

Norwegian refugees.

121

The *Hessa* arrived on the spot and the two submarines, and their crew of one man for each sub, were put over the side along with the two rubber dinghies with stores and mines for their operation. The *Hessa* then put to sea again landing back at base.

The next trip was to the isle of Hitra, the trip starting on the 13th and ending on 15th of September. On this trip the *Hessa* was towing a small fishing boat that had a lot of stuff onboard. The boat did not have enough speed to get over from Shetland to Norway in a short enough time, so we got the job to tow the boat over at a speed of 13 knots. The weather was very fine. The tow was released when the fishing boat was about 15 miles off the coast where the boat had to steam into. The *Hessa* then went back to base, nothing unusual being seen.

On the 18th we set off to an isle near Frøysjøen, and were back next day. We had onboard three men and a lot of stores. There was light rain when we came near the entrance of the bay where the stuff was to be put ashore. The sparky was just about to switch the radio off when he heard the calling code for the *Hessa*, so he listened and got the message. He turned the radio off then ran up to the top bridge and handed the message to the skipper. The message was, "SC *Hessa* do not go into the bay as there are three German E-boats waiting for you. Return to base."

The skipper could see the three E-boats, lying in such a position that they could fire at the *Hessa* without getting in the firing line of each other. The passage was too narrow for the *Hessa* to turn around so we had to go astern for nearly a quarter of a mile, then head back to base.

On our way back to Shetland, steaming on a westerly course, about 5am the lookout spotted something like a conning tower, about half a mile away on our starboard side. So the ship was put on action station and all guns were turned towards the object. The first shell to hit the target was from the Bofors gun, then the Oerlikon and the six-pounder cannon had a hit. The Bofors crew fired about six shots, each was a hit, but it was the six-pounder that got three shots near the waterline and sank the thing.

The object had a number 24 on its side and it was not a conning tower but a big buoy. It was the same thing that we had seen on a previous trip. The buoy had been attached to a submarine net which was drifting in the North Sea. Now the net went to the bottom and out of harm's way for the sub-chasers and M.T.B.s. After the sinking the *Hessa* steamed back to base.

On 22nd September our next trip was to the isle of Skorpa, south of Ålesund, with two men and a lot of stores. The trip was succesful. The wind was southerly moderate to fresh. Back at base we had a few days rest.

The next trip was on 1st and 2nd October. This was to a place called Klufti i Fensfjord. We had two men and some stores on board. On the trip into Klufti the lookout spotted a German destroyer cruising slowly along the firth which the *Hessa* had to cross to arrive at Klufti. So we had to take a slow trip around the isles to avoid being spotted by the Germans. The destroyer steamed away and the *Hessa* landed the men with their gear, and then returned to base.

On our trip back to base, at 3.55am, the ship just about jumped out of the water. We heard six heavy explosions. Everything on the starboard side came in like an avalanche and landed down in the port side of the ship and all the lights went out. But the engine was still running at 1500 rpm. It took a few minutes before the engineers got the power back to the alarm system, and in that time one man in the fo'c'sle went up to have a look. All he could see was a rush of seawater over the deck, so he went down again. One man asked what had caused the explosions, and the answer was that it must have been a mine which had blown up just alongside the ship.

He went back to his bunk but he did not get a chance to turn in before the alarm sounded and the boys went to their action stations. They sighted a plane coming in on our starboard side. The gun crew opened up with the guns which were able to fire on the plane. It got a good few hits so it went nearly straight up and disappeared. We did not see the plane again. We were surprised to notice markings on it like those of the R.A.F. The main radio was out of order after the terrible shaking, but the wireless operator had an emergency radio. He tried that out and sent a message to our radio station at Scapa Flow. He said the *Hessa* had been bombed by a plane with R.A.F. markings and that the ship had taken in a lot of sea water but was still steaming at 15 knots. The wind was then south-westerly about force eight or nine. When the six explosions were heard we thought that a German destroyer was shelling us, but after we had seen the plane we knew that it had been either bombs or depth charges which had been dropped on us.

When we were about 20 nautical miles east of Sumburgh Head the radio operator got a question from Sumburgh Airport asking if we wanted an escort by an R.A.F. plane. The skipper answered that he would not take the responsibility of what the gun crew would do if any plane came within gun range. If they were to send out a plane it should not come nearer than one and a half nautical miles. We spotted two planes but they kept a good distance from us.

When the *Hessa* steamed into Scalloway I was up on deck and found a piece of iron. When I examined it I noticed the British Government mark and number. I took it up to the bridge and handed it to the skipper and he took care of it. *Hessa* was moored along the jetty and we got a portable pump onboard to pump out the water, it was more than three and a half feet deep at the fore end. We got all the seawater pumped out and repaired the bilge suction line. The line was broken off at the steel bulkhead. When that was done, and not a drop of seawater came into the bilges, the *Hessa* was put on the slipway. The fore part was inspected and it was found that nine planks on the starboard side were cracked between the two steel bulkheads. Five planks were cracked on the port side between two bulkheads. When the *Hessa* steamed through the bolt of depth charges she got four on the starboard side and two on the port side.

The *Hessa* then steamed to Peterhead to go on the slipway for repairs.

The work was done in reasonable time and the planks that had been damaged were replaced. We then came back to Scalloway and got assigned to take a trip to a place called Follesvåg near Austevoll. The trip started on 20th November. We were lying about four nautical miles off the coast, then came close to the coast about noon. But the *Hessa* had got a new skipper and he did not know the coast there. The men in charge and most of the crew knew the coast, and they were not very happy about the position just outside one of the coastal watch posts. We moved a bit closer so the distance from the ship to shore was only about three nautical miles. When you put your binoculars on and spied towards the German watch tower you could see the soldiers walking around.

At 4.30pm that afternoon the *Hessa* steamed into the fjord known as Korsfjord some miles west of Bergen. The crew made all the guns ready, tommy guns, stenguns and hand grenades, just to be ready if the Germans did send out gunboats. When the *Hessa* passed the German watch tower about three quarters of a mile away, it was a bit dark and the Germans then morsed a message to the main coastal fort at the head of Korsfjord. The message was sent in clear language – "Enemy gunboat entering the fjord."

We then steamed to a small isle, went alongside the rock face and moored up. The time was now about 5pm and *Hessa* was supposed to be there before 7, as the man we were to meet there was not to come before 7.15, to collect stores and other stuff. The skipper said that he wanted two men on watch, one on the bridge and one on deck. The watches were only 30 minutes each. At 7pm the watch-keeper heard machine gun fire and we were worried that the Germans had captured our contact man and helpers. It was then decided to stay put till 8pm.

I had just been down in the engine room to check over the temperatures and so on. When I came back on deck I met the second in charge. He said that he hoped our contact man and helpers had not been caught. We were standing outside the wheelhouse when we heard the faint creak of oars in the rowlock of a rowing boat. We went to the ship's side and spotted a boat with three men. We could hear them discussing if the *Hessa* had arrived. The second in charge called out for the password, and he got the reply, "Jakob er hjemme (Jakob is at home)." He then told them to come alongside. The rowing boat was only about 15 or 18 feet from the *Hessa* but they could not see her as she was lying in deep shadows of the small isle.

The three men came onboard and we took them down to the mess room for a meal of bacon, eggs bread and strong coffee. The crew of the *Hessa* then put the stores up on deck. There was some rubber containers ready to be sunk at a convenient place, with about two fathoms between the containers on a rope. At 8.15pm all was clear and the rowing boat left, and so did *Hessa*, but she steamed out toward sea on a different channel. Everything was quiet, just a little breeze. We had cleared the outermost isles and rocks by about 9pm when the fun started from the big fort at Korsfjord, the Korsnes fort. We did not know what they were shooting at. It was not at the *Hessa* but we could see the gun flashes after midnight. We steamed at 15 knots so were about 45 miles to the west when we saw the last gun flash.

The passage back to Scalloway was very fine, and *Hessa* arrived about 8.30 in the morning of 21st November, 1944. Just after we came alongside the quay the officers onboard came to congratulate us on a successful trip. They told us that we could put six swastikas on the front of the bridge, as the Germans had seen us moving at Korsfjord and then lost contact. A small German coaster came steaming from somewhere among the isles and the German fort started shelling the coaster and then the four armed German trawlers turned in and shot at the coaster. The coaster only had a small machine gun and was soon sunk. After this came a German troop transport ship and the German trawlers opened fire on her. The Korsnes fort opened up and the result was four trawlers, one small coaster of 900 tonnes and the troop transport ship with 250-300 troops – all sunk. I was sounding the fuel tanks when I heard this news so I said that we had never fired a single shot on that trip so that was economy warfare, to get the enemy to sink its own ships.

Now the *Hessa's* crew had a few days out among the isles, practising with the guns on a target which was towed by a spitfire fighting plane. We were out practising for about three hours and then back to Scalloway. On 26th November we got orders to take a trip with two men to be put ashore at Hovda Frøysjøen. The trip went fine and we arrived at the appointed place and got the men ashore with their stores. Then the wind freshened up to gale forceand when *Hessa* got out on the fjord two German E-boats came chasing us. The skipper gave order to run with the breaking sea and increase the revs on the engine from 1500 to 1960 rpm, and the German E-boats gave up the chase. The man who was at the engine control just pushed the throttle forward and then noticed that the rpm was over 2100. Then a big sea arose on port quarter and lifted the ship with the result that she got her bow buried in solid sea. The man at the controls then eased back the throttle to 1500rpm and the *Hessa* got clear of the heavy seas. We did not see the German E-boats again and went back on course for Shetland.

We arrived in Lerwick on 28th November and went ashore. Looking back at the *Hessa* we noticed that the after-part had a twist to starboard. We went up ahead of the vessel and noticed the bow was twisted on port. So the *Hessa* was now out of service again and had to go back to the slipway at Peterhead. When she came on the slipway and was inspected, it was found that the larch planking which had been used to repair the damage caused by the depth-charges, did not stand up to the strain in bad weather, and new planking had to be put in. She also got two extra steel bulkheads as stiffening to prevent more damage if the *Hessa* should run into bad weather again.

CHAPTER NINE

Marriage and Peace

I had a short time off when I got married on 6th December, 1944. My bride was a Scalloway girl, Cissie Slater, whom I had seen on several occasions in the forces canteen, in what used to be the United Free Church up near the school. One night she attended a function in Norway House and I asked her if I could see her home. That was the start of our romance.

We were married in Scalloway Church of Scotland by the Rev Park Jones. Our best man was another Norwegian, Harald Sulstad and best maid was a Scalloway lady, Margaret Hughson. The reception was held in Scalloway Public Hall, which by that time was no longer used as a hospital. We had well over 300 guests and it was a night to remember. They granted me a day of work the following day.

Then I was asked to go on the *Vigra* as chief engineer. We went round to Lerwick to await orders to go to Norway. The refugees we were to pick up had not all got together until 21st December, then we got the order to go. We left on 23rd December and were back next day. We went to Follesvåg, where the *Hessa* had been some weeks before, and where the Germans had panicked and sunk six of their own ships. On this trip we learned that the fishermen in that area got 100 Norwegian kroner for any dead soldier who had leather boots and a greatcoat on, whereas they got only 25 to 50 kroner for dead soldiers who had only a uniform and rubber boots. They had to put the bodies ashore on rocks or isles and then notify the German police, stating the numbers in full and part uniform.

Kaare and Cissie on their wedding day, 6th December, 1944. © C. J. Williamson.

We got all the refugees and started back for Shetland. We had 19 refugees from Bergen, including five women. Three of the women got bunks in the mess room and went straight to lie down. The other two just sat in the mess room and told us how much food they had bought on the black market. When they decided to escape they locked all their windows and doors so nobody could get in to steal their food and other valuable items. When I came down to the mess room for a coffee they were still there going bla-bla-bla.

One of them was violently sick over the mess table. I asked one of the boys to clean up and then told the woman that she wasn't sea-sick – it was the effect of a big meal that she had had.

I told her that there was a toilet 16 feet from where she was sitting and she should go there and be sick. I also told her that we would not arrive in Lerwick before 4pm so we would not have much of a chance to clear up the mess deck before we had our Christmas meal. I also told her that we were risking ship and crew for people like her and that I believed that she and her family were not in any danger from the Germans.

Well she gave me a blast, telling me that I was just a common seaman, that she was married to a very rich merchant man and she was going to report me to the skipper. I just had to give her an answer so I said, "You call me a common seaman but you and the rest of your black market friends had to call for help from a ship manned with common seamen." There was no comment and she went to bed.

The trip was very smooth, hardly any movement on the ship. The *Vigra* arrived in Lerwick at 4pm. The refugees went ashore and I was sounding the fuel tanks just where the gangway was. They thanked us for the trip and wished us a Merry Christmas and so on. Then my lady friend came sailing along in a new fur coat with the collar up. You could hardly see her face or the top of her head. When she was about halfway across the gangway, I said to her, "I bid you welcome to Lerwick and I wish you a Merry Christmas and a Happy New Year." She turned and saw me and said, "Thank you." Then she sailed ashore.

The skipper was standing outside the wheelhouse door and he came and told me that she had put in a complaint about me. I said that she was the only one who caused trouble and that she had called me a common seaman. The skipper had heard the story from the other woman and agreed that it did not correspond with the complaint she gave to him. We did our best to clean up the mess deck and the rest of the ship before 6pm, and then we had our Christmas dinner.

I then went to Scalloway to have Christmas with my wife. On Christmas Day I got transport from Scalloway to Lerwick. The skipper who was on the trip stopped in Scalloway and before I left he told me to tell the second in charge to take the *Vigra* to Scalloway that day.

I arrived onboard and told the second in charge the message, but he said that he had not heard anything from the skipper. I asked him if he had been ashore and made any enquiries about what to do. He replied that he had not been ashore because he could not leave the ship without an officer. I said that he had two quarter-masters who had more experience with running the ship and handling the crew. I told him that he was a pig-headed fool and that he thought that he could do just what he wanted because he was a son of a Norwegian ship owner. I asked why he had not given the crew their Christmas drink. He answered that the crew did not deserve to get the drink. After that the quarter-master and I demanded the drink, so he had to dish it out much against his will.

I got transport back to Scalloway and reported to the skipper what took place onboard the *Vigra*. He said that he was going to Lerwick early the next morning and added that I did not have to come. He said that the first and second engineers would have to take the *Vigra* back to Scalloway. She arrived in Scalloway at 10am on 26th December. After re-fuelling we had some trips outside Scalloway practising firing at targets towed by a Spitfire. I was finished onboard the *Vigra* on 10th of February.

I worked in the stores for the sub-chasers until I was ordered to go onboard the *Hitra* as first engineer, on a trip to Follesvøg, my third trip to that place, with five tonnes of explosives, small arms and ammunition. The trip started on 15th January, 1945 and finished in the afternoon of the 16th. The trip was long enough for me as I was watch keeping engineer before the trip started. The trip started at 3am and I should have been released from watch at 4am. But no relieving engineer turned up to do their watch, so I just kept watch. 8am came and then I was expecting the chief engineer would come down to the control room. But no. I then asked one of the deck crew to bring me a cup of coffee but I did not get any coffee, so I had to drink cold water and chew dry biscuits. To cut it short I was on watch from 8am of the 14th and when the ship came near the Norwegian coast it was put on action station. I had to be on watch but none of the other engineers nor the chief engineer showed their faces down in the engine room.

We arrived at Follesvøg and moored up to a fishing boat so now it was clear ship. I took a chance to leave the engine room to go to the mess room to get myself a cup of coffee and a sandwich. When I came on deck I met two of the engineers and the electrician. I asked the engineers if they were passengers or engineers on a pleasure trip. Then one of the quarter-masters asked who was down in the engine room. One of the engineers said that I was the watch keeper. The quarter-master told me to go back to the engine room so I told him that I had been on watch from when the ship left Shetland and had not had any food for the whole trip until now, so I was going down to the mess room to get a cup of coffee and some sandwiches. When I came down to the mess room I saw the chief engineer sitting speaking to a Norwegian from the shore. I made some sandwiches and a cup of coffee and went back on stand by watch.

All the cargo was put onboard the fishing boat and the *Hitra* started the voyage back to Shetland at 2 am. I started my second long watch and neither the chief engineer nor any of the other three engineers showed their faces in the engine room. I finally got a cup of coffee about 9am and the *Hitra* arrived in Scalloway about 2pm on the 16th January. When you add up the time I was on watch it was a total of 60 hours.

When we came back to Scalloway I told the chief engineer that he and his bloody nig-nog of engineers were what they used to put on the garbage dump. They got called engineers but they did not have a clue what an engineer was. I was appointed to be a reserve chief engineer for the three sub-chasers' so-called engineers, but so far I had not seen any onboard the *Hitra*. The chief engineer said that he was very sorry. I answered that the least he could have done was to come down to the control room and let me go and have a meal that I was entitled to get, instead of staying in his bunk.

I got the impression that the engineers were jealous because the *Hessa* could put up six swastikas on her bridge. I told the skipper that I would not make another trip on the *Hitra* but he pleaded with me to make another trip because he could not get another engineer from the base in Scalloway. There were no fewer than six of them, but some were nervous and others had some other excuses. There was one who complained of diesel eczema so he could not go. I noticed he could wash engine parts in diesel oil without any trouble.

I was called to go on another trip with the *Hitra* to a place called Fensfjord. It started on 18th January and we were back the next day. The trip across from Shetland went well, and I had only two watches on the crossing. When we came close to the Norwegian coast the ship was put on action stations. As first engineer I had to be on watch in the control room, and as usual none of the other engineers came into the control room. As it happened my watch started after we had left and the ship was all clear. We picked up two men who had finished their job in Norway to go back to their respective training camps. I did my watch and to my surprise the chief engineer came down to the control room and asked if everything was working right. I said it was and that having finished my watch I wanted a relief so I could go and have a cup of coffee. He promised to tell the engineer who had the watch after me to turn to and take his watch, but he never appeared, so I had to keep watch for another four hours. It was a fine trip with hardly any movement or rolling.

I did the next watch but nobody came near the control room. So I had now been on watch for 18 hours and I can tell you that I was not in a very good mood. At 12 midday I left the engine room and went aft to the mess room and asked the chief engineer why he had not got any of the ship's engineers to come and take their watches so I could get some food. He told me that he had told one of the engineers to go and take the watch so that I could be relieved. I told the chief that the whole engine crew were a bunch of bastards and I was not going down to carry on the watch before I had some food – and maybe not then either. I got my food and then I went down to the control room to continue the watch as none of the other so-called engineers would do so. I was on watch until the *Hitra* arrived in Scalloway.

I was working ashore and then I was called back to the *Hitra* for another trip to a place called Lyngøy in Hjelme outside Bergen. The trip started on 24th January and finished the next day. *Hitra* left Scalloway at 3pm with a westerly breeze which was not bad for the trip. As usual I had the harbour watch, and this time the sea watches started at 4am. As I had the last harbour watch I had to take the first sea watch till 8am, but as usual onboard the *Hitra* none of the so-called engineers turned up to take their watch.

So there I went once more on a long stretch of watches. I was on watch when we left Scalloway and now at 12 midnight I had not seen either the chief engineer or any of the engine crew. But this time I was prepared. I had brought some beer to take with me so in that way it was okay. But I would have preferred a cup of coffee. I had fresh water, so I did not trouble any of the engine crew.

The crossing went fine and the *Hitra* arrived at the appointed place at the right time. After the *Hitra* had moored up to a fishing boat and started to discharge the cargo I went up to go to the mess deck to get a cup of coffee. I was going to the mess deck when the coxswain – the same one who had been on a previous trip – told me to go back to the control room and stand by. I told him that there were another four engineers onboard so he could tell them to go down to take a watch as I had been on watch since the ship left Shetland. I was going to have a good cup of coffee and something to eat. I had my coffee and I had words with the chief engineeer and I also had a talk with the commanding officer. He promised to talk to the chief engineer but it was no use. *Hitra* started on the trip back to Shetland and I started on a continual watch.

When we were about 30 or 40 miles east of Sumburgh Head the *Hitra* ran into blinding snow showers. The captain decided to shelter in Sandwick Bay where we arrived about 2pm and dropped anchor. We lay there for two hours, then raised the anchor and steamed for Scalloway, arriving there about 6pm. When the ship was moored up I took my gear and made ready to go ashore. The chief engineer then came and told me to sound the fuel tanks and wash down the main engines as I was to have the harbour watch. Well there was some nasty language which came between the chief engineer and myself.

I went home and the following day the sparky came up to the house with a message from the chief engineer to return to the *Hitra*. I told him that I had a very bad cold and that I was not coming back. I had peace for a couple of days, then I got a visit from the officers of the base along with the commanding officer of the *Hitra* and he ordered me to go back on her as first engineer. I just told him and the other officer why I refused to go back, and that I had a very bad cold. I was then told to go to the Norwegian hospital in Lerwick. I agreed to that, but the officer would have to drive me to hospital as there was no taxi in Scalloway. Transport from the office was laid on for 10am, and whoever was to drive me into Lerwick had to come to the house and pick me up.

During the night it had been snowing pretty heavy so the small car which was to be used was changed to a small army truck. At the Norwegian surgery I was told to strip off above the belt so that the assistant could sound my chest. I was told to take two deep breaths and cough. Every time I coughed he made a cross on the back and front of my chest. Then he said to me, "Sailor, you have tuberculosis. Just put your clothes back on again." I started to do so and then the surgeon jumped up from his chair at the desk and started to sound my chest. He said that I had a bad case of bronchitis and he told the young doctor to clean off all the crosses he had marked on my chest and back. The surgeon then gave me a line to present to the X-ray department at the hospital. I got my X-ray result two days later. It was clear.

I was now working ashore as there were no trips to make to Norway. The *Vigra* had made one trip after the *Hitra's* last trip. There was a lot of snow and bad weather on the Norwegian coast, so that had put a stop to the sabotage work along the coast. I had to go to the dentist one day and when I came back to Scalloway I saw that the *Hessa* had arrived from Peterhead where she had been for repairs. I did not go home right away but went onboard the *Hessa* and talked to the crew. The following morning I joined the *Hessa* and worked there as first engineeer along with the other engine room crew.

The *Hessa* did not get a trip until the 12th of January to a place called Torkildsvøgen, at Bømlo. We had two men to put ashore along with a lot of explosives, ammunition and stores. The *Hessa* started on the trip back to Scalloway with moderate weather all the way. On the trip over a U-boat surfaced about 500 yards astern of the *Hessa*. It just broke the surface and dived right away so we could not see the number on the conning tower. The commander on the U-boat likely had a big surprise. We did not see it again. We arrived back at Scalloway in the afternoon of the 13th. We then did some gun practice shooting at targets with our Oerlikons outside Scalloway.

The *Hessa's* next trip was to Arot in Fensfjord. We left Scalloway at 2am with a fresh south-west breeze, and very cold. When we were about 30 miles from the Norwegian coast the lookout on the bridge spotted one plane and when it had passed the *Hessa* the pilot, or whoever it was, fired parachute flashes so the area around us was well lit up. That happened twice more. The plane left us and we got to the isles where the three men were waiting to be taken onboard. They could see the *Hessa* very clearly. Our job was completed and the *Hessa* steamed back to Scalloway, arriving at 4pm of the 22nd January.

The next trip was to Kjelnesvik. It started at 2am on the 4th March. The *Hessa* got a good following wind, mostly gale force from west-south-west and arrived at the appointed place to put ashore two men with their stores etc. When that was done we left for Scalloway. The wind was now a full gale and the *Hessa* had to have a man standing by with the controls. He had to ease the throttle back until the ship was on top of the breaker then give the recommended revs. The man at the controls was changed every 30 minutes. All went well and we arrived in Scalloway at 4pm on 5th March.

Our next trip was to Slott in Sunnhordland on the 8th of March. We left Scalloway at 3am with two men, some stores and ammunition. The trip went very well with a calm, smooth sea. We were back at Scalloway at 2pm the next day. On this trip I noticed a strange sound from the port side engine. I could not find out what was causing it so I reported it to the chief engineer. He came onboard and I started the engine so he could hear the sound, but he could not find out what or where it came from.

It was time for another trip to Arøy. I had been there before. On this trip we had two men to put ashore with stores and ammunition. I asked if the shore chief engineer could come on this trip, so we could maybe locate the trouble. The trip went fine and the men were put ashore with all their stuff. The *Hessa* arrived back at Scalloway on the 16th March, 1945. I was then to take the port engine ashore, strip it down and also overhaul it, and then overhaul the starboard engine. The port engine was taken to an unused store and there it was rigged up to a tripod so it could be hoisted up so the engineers could walk around it. All 16 cylinders were taken over to the workshop to be cleaned and done up.

One day the engineer came to the place where the engine hung and I was trying the crankshaft for end float (slack up or down) when I found that there was too much clearance. I told the engineer officer what I had found. So one of the engine room crew and I stripped off the gearbox and the engineer officer said that he would bet five pounds that we would not find anything wrong there. When the gearbox was sitting on the floor we found out what the trouble was. It was a thrust bearing which was worn down 65,000th of an inch. That was the cause of the sound we heard. We replaced the thrust bearing, overhauled the engine and put it back onboard the *Hessa*. But I did not get my five pound bet from the engineer officer.

After both her engines were overhauled we went out on a trial run and then the *Hessa* had a trip to a place called Torkildsvågen, at the isle of Bømlo. The trip started on 27th March, to land two men and a lot of ammunition and stores. The weather was fine and no strange sound came from the engine. This was a quick trip of just over 28 hours. It was also very successful because when *Hessa* came into the pick-up place, the contact man was there, so our two men just had to step off the *Hessa* and board the fishing boat which was to bring them to their destination.

The next trip was on 5th April when the *Hessa* had to pick up two men who had finished their job in Norway. Back in Scalloway the *Hessa* did only routine work such as gun practice. There wasn't much work to be done, just waiting patiently. We would surely get a trip soon as the sailing season was fast coming to an end. The three sub-chasers did not sail to Norway in the summertime owing to the short night. If a boat came into an isle to land men, ammo or stores, it was easy for any nosey quisling, or others who sided with the Germans – they were called stripes – to see us. The men or women who were called stripes were some of the worst to spread stories about what they had seen. But in many a case it was just malicious stories so that the bastards could be at the centre of attention. But it did not do them any good, quite the opposite. Most of the people along the coast, who had contact with the *Hessa, Hitra* and *Vigra* did not believe the stories which circulated in some parts of the coast.

After more practice work *Hessa* got a trip to an island near Bømlo, called Nautøy, to put two men ashore there with ammunition and stores. The trip went fine with good weather so it lasted only 28 hours. Back in Scalloway there wasn't much doing apart from practice with guns on targets which were being towed by Spitfires. At Scalloway the ship was painted with camouflage paint.

On 23rd April, *Hessa* got a trip to a place called Storesund. We landed three men with the usual ammunition and stores. The trip was very fine – not a breath of wind and the sea as smooth as a table top. We landed our men and returned to Scalloway the next day.

On the morning of the 8th May came the news that the Germans had surrendered over the whole of Europe. The three sub-chasers fired their parachute rockets and the loud speakers were turned on full. The weather was nearly calm so the people of Scalloway had music while they worked. In the afternoon the officers of the unit came onboard the *Hessa* to listen to Mr. Churchill and also to have a drink with the crew. The officers, Major Rodgers, Captain Lieutenant H. Hendriksen and Captain De Bertodano wanted to see the six-pounder gun in operation, so the gunner went into the gun turret and fired five shots at the hill on the east side of Scalloway.

At night there was a dance and a bonfire, not to forget the beer and rum, so I suppose that there were quite a few sore heads the next day. We didn't worry about self-inflicted injury, that would likely right itself in its own time.

Now the crew of the three sub-chasers started to buy stuff to take over to Norway. We managed to get coffee, white flour, soap, sewing thread and leather for mending boots. The *Hessa's* first trip after the war finished was to an outlying place called Øklandsvågen, to discharge 20 barrels of diesel oil for the resistance group there. After that was discharged we steamed back to the village of Rubbestadneset where the chief engineer came from and where the Shetland Bus fishing boats got engine spares from during the war.

When the *Hessa* arrived at Rubbestadneset the people there had got word from Øklandsvågen, so all who could walk or crawl were on the quayside when the ship arrived. I was up on deck when we came alongside and I heard a voice which said, "Are you here Johan?" I went down to the control room to be ready to stop the main engine but the ship got a bad list to port. Before I got the signal to stop the main engine the port side engine was choked with its own exhaust, because the outlet was about three feet below the surface as so many people from shore came onboard.

There was no damage done and the people spread out. Some went down to the mess deck and quite a few came down to the engine room to have a good look at our engine, as most of the men there were working in Norway's biggest motor factory, the Wichmann Motor Factory.

Some of the crew of the *Hessa* asked if it was possible to get some small birch or rowan plants to take back to Scalloway. We got small trees, some just a foot high, with the roots and some earth along with

Hessa in Ålesund, 14th May, 1945. Just after arrival when the people discovered that there was a Norwegian gunboat which had arrived, the first of the Norwegian Naval Unit.

each plant. There were rowan, birch and spruce. I do not know how many plants there were, but there were three or four boxes. The *Hessa* stopped there for nearly three hours and then we were ready to push off. We were delayed because we had to have a big birch tree to bring back to Scalloway. Three young men came with the tree which was 12 or 15 feet high. The birch was then secured to the starboard rail and the *Hessa* started on the return trip. Just before we arrived in Scalloway the crew of the Bofors gun took the tree and lashed it to the barrel and then they elevated it right up so the people of Scalloway could see the tree. Then they took branches off it and planted them in some gardens in Scalloway. Quite a lot of the branches took root and were growing fine.

That was the first trip to Norway after the German surrender. When the *Hessa* was a Rubbestadneset the crew of two German patrol boats which were lying there did not really understand what to do. The Germans did not come closer to the *Hessa* than about 100 yards. They looked like people who had lost all the arrogance that they used to have. Now they seemed subdued with not a shout or bawl to be heard as had been the usual way. Now they were just a bunch of frightened men without a leader.

Back at Scalloway our crew went on another shopping spree. We bought flour, coffee and a lot of things which were not on ration books – cigarettes, tobacco, soap and so on. The next trip was to Ålesund. It started on the 14th of May in smashing sunshine that continued when the *Hessa* arrived at Ålesund. The ship was at action stations as there was a good number of German patrol boats and mine sweepers tied up there. Our commanding officer thought it was best to be prepared. When the *Hessa* came alongside the quay we saw a lot of people who lined both sides of the street. Then we spotted an open car driving along the street slowly with a man standing in it. He was the quisling leader for Alesund so when the car passed the office he had raised his arm in a Hitler salute. Then a man from the crowd ran up to the car and pushed the bastard down. The quisling leader was then put into prison.

Top and middle: Party for the *Hessa* crew together with men from the
Homefront at Ålesund, 15th May, 1945.
Bottom: Passengers on the bridge with the Aft gun on the *Hessa*,
15th May, 1945.

The people of Ålesund noticed the *Hessa* but did not realise at first that it was a Norwegian ship. But when they found out, it was nearly impossible for the crew to get ashore. As soon as you were on the quay you were attacked by old ladies and young women kissing and embracing. That had to come to an end so the crew members who were not on duty went on parade along with the men of the resistance group. I was on duty so I could not attend. When the crew were on parade I had quite a lot of visitors onboard. In the engine room and also down in the mess deck I was dishing out cups of coffee, so I was not lonely.

In the evening the crew of the *Hessa* and the crew of two motor torpedo boats which arrived some time in the afternoon, were invited to a dinner at the town hall, along with the resistance officers and merchants of Ålesund. The following day, the 16th, the crew was walking around the town and met a lot of Russian prisoners-of-war who were given cigarettes from our boys. As it was the day before the 17th of May, Norwegian Independence Day, the commanding officer sent a telegram to London with a request to stop over in Ålesund to celebrate the day. We received the answer, "Return to base at 6pm in the evening." Well the crew of the *Hessa* was not in a good mood but an order was an order, so we left Ålesund at the right time.

When the *Hessa* came into Scalloway at 8am on 17th May we did not see the other two sub-chasers. We were wondering if this boat would be going to Lerwick because the *Hitra* and the *Vigra* were ordered to go to Bergen. When we asked about them the answer was that they were ordered back to base. They arrived in the late afternoon of the 19th of May with a reduced crew. The *Hitra* had an American deck officer with them, and was also missing the two commanding officers on the *Hitra*. *Vigra* got a reprimand for not only disobeying orders, but leaving some of the crew in Bergen.

The *Hessa* got orders to take a trip to a village called Leirvik, on the isle of Stord, with some stuff which belonged to one of the engineers who came from that village. We left Scalloway on the evening of the

26th May and arrived about 11am on the Sunday morning. The people of the village were walking to church when they saw the camouflaged ship come steaming into the harbour, and then they noticed the Norwegian navy flag, so they about-turned and came down to the quay. The only ones who were left at the church were the minister and the bell ringer. As the minister said later on, there was no use holding a sermon in an empty church so he and the bell ringer also came to the quay, talked to the crew and invited us to a remembrance ceremony at the church. Most of the crew went, but as usual I, as duty engineer, had to stop onboard.

When I was down in the engine room someone shouted down and asked if anybody was onboard. When I came up on deck I met a man and he asked if he could get coffee. I took him down to the mess deck and made him a jug of coffee. He gave me a strange look and then he said that he wanted dry coffee as his daughter had a christening party. I gave him a small bag of coffee and he asked me to come up to his house but I could not leave the ship. He said he would come back later which he did. I went up to his house and then I found out what sort of people I had given the coffee to – a bloody bunch of Nazi bastards. I asked them why they did not get coffee and stores from the damned Krauts. I also said that I hoped the whole lot of them choked on the coffee and then I left and went back to the *Hessa* in not a very good mood.

In the evening the whole crew of the *Hessa* were invited to a party arranged by the resistance group at Leirvik. The meal consisted of fresh lobster, salad and bread. Each of the crew took a girl to the party. The party lasted until midnight, then we had to escort our partners home. Then back to the *Hessa* and back to Scalloway. We arrived at Scalloway about 9am. All was well.

This was one of the last trips that the Hessa did from Scalloway to Norway. It was sort of a sad feeling on the last trip from Scalloway, as we had got to know the people there. They saw when the fishing boats left and kept watching until the boat arrived back. They also noticed when

Parade of the Homefront and the *Hessa* men at Ålesund on 15th May, 1945.

some of the boats did not return. Everyone in Scalloway and Burra had a good idea what was going on but never a question was asked about where the missing crew and boat had gone. I suppose that they knew.

I will end by saying, "Thank you" to the people of Scalloway and Burra. Thank you for all you did for us and God bless you all.

Kaare and his wife, Cissie. © C. J. Williamson.

Kaare meet the Queen. From left: Captain W. Coutts, Dr. J. R. Durham,
Captain L. Hardy, Kaare Iversen, Queen Elizabeth II
and Sir Basil Neven Spence. © C. J. Williamson.

Cissie and Kaare, 1963. © C. J. Williamson.

Kaare, Cissie and family, 1963. © C. J. Williamson.

Kaare Iversen. Photo © Trygve Sørvaag.

Other titles of interest from The Shetland Times Ltd.

The Shetland Bus by David Howarth

1 898852 42 1 – £7.99 – Pbk
The classic story of secret wartime
missions across the North Sea.

Shetland Bus Faces and Places 60 Years On by Trygve Sørvaag

1 898852 88 X – £25.00 – Hbk
A vivid description of two coastal communities
and a new perspective on our wartime history.

Willie's War and Other Stories by Willie Smith

1 898852 97 9 – £9.99 – Pbk
Wartime memories of the Shetland Bus boys
and life in Scalloway during the war.

Available from:

71-79 Commercial Street, Lerwick, Shetland ZE1 0AJ
Tel: 01595 695531   Fax: 01595 692897
E-mail: bookshop@shetland-times.co.uk
www.shetland-bookshop.co.uk

Member of the Booksellers Association